MURDER MOST BIZARRE

NICK FLETCHER is a former crime reporter and the author of a series of novels and short stories about ex-journalist turned private detective Max Slater.

As a journalist, Nick worked alongside police on many murder hunts in the Midlands and covered the sensational trial of child-killer Raymond Morris, known as 'The Monster Of Cannock Chase' and reported extensively on the hunt for 'Black Panther' Donald Neilson who shot dead three men and kidnapped and murdered a young student, Lesley Whittle.

Years later, Nick Fletcher had a much more personal encounter with murder, assisting Scotland Yard detectives with background information when a friend was brutally killed. Two men were convicted of the murder and given life sentences.

Nick Fletcher lives in South Devon where he works as a freelance writer.

GW00566959

NICK FLETCHER

MURDER
MOST
BIZARRE

CB
Classic Books

Published by Classic Books
TQ5 0HG

Printed in Great Britain by TJ Books,
Padstow, Cornwall

British Library Cataloguing in Publication Data.
A catalogue record for this book is available from the British Library

ISBN 978-0-9519399-2-5

Contents

A Question Of Motive   1

The Man On The Roof   11

The Farmhouse Murders   19

The Second Shot   25

Confession   33

The Reluctant Judge   41

The Acid Test   47

Death On Wheels   57

The Secret Trial   65

Cheating The Hangman   75

The Seductive Wife   81

The Mystery Man   89

The Body In The Trunk   95

Brainstorm   103

Judge And Jury   109

INTRODUCTION

The murder cases featured in this book are spread across the south coast of England and span the period from the 1900s to the 1950s, a time when police methods and forensic science were still developing, when CCTV and the internet were just futuristic concepts and when it was much easier to get away with murder than it is today in our closely-monitored society.

The cases I have selected are not necessarily the most gruesome nor the most notorious, but they are certainly among the most extraordinary, either in the nature of the crime, the characteristics of the killer, the motivation, or the eventual outcome.

Murder is a chilling word for callous and often brutal killings, which are horrific crimes wherever they may take place but strangely more unsettling when they are located in or around seaside resorts, places created to provide happiness and carefree pleasures. The warm climate, blue sky and blue sea of England's south coast attracts not just holiday-makers but a variety of criminals who see potentially easy pickings among people frequently off-guard when enjoying themselves. Travelling from London and from towns and cities within easy reach of the coast, these criminals are mostly petty thieves, pickpockets, fraudsters and drug-pushers. And some are murderers.

People capable of committing murder are spread right across the social scale and can often include outwardly respectable professions such as doctors and lawyers. Yet whatever the social status of the murderer, their crimes are most commonly motivated by greed, jealousy, revenge - and sometimes what appears to be pure evil.

My own interest in murder was sparked in August 1965 when just weeks after becoming a trainee reporter at a Wolverhampton Press agency, I left my office to get some lunch and within a few yards found myself at the scene of a crime which had happened just moments earlier. Slumped in a shop doorway, a uniformed police officer was bleeding from stab wounds. A small crowd was gathering and within minutes the area was swamped by police searching for the killer. An ambulance arrived to tend to the police officer, but it was too late. He died on his way to the hospital.

The officer, Detective Sergeant Jim Stanford, was aged 40 and married with three children. He knew he was fatally wounded and just before he died, he was able to name his killer. He said the man who stabbed him was 19-year-old David Henry Wardley, who was on the run from Borstal and having been recognised by Sergeant Stanford, stabbed the officer while being questioned. Wardley was arrested a few hours later after being found in the nearby Gaumont cinema having boasted to someone that he was the man 'who done the copper'. Wardley was convicted of murder and given the death penalty but it was commuted to a life sentence.

Just a few weeks later, I had another stark reminder of the tragedy and the consequences of murder when I watched a judge at Stafford Assizes put on the black cap – actually a square of black material – and pass the death sentence on a convicted killer. The sentence was again commuted to life imprisonment as the death sentence was due to be abolished just a few months later. I had witnessed one of the last occasions a judge would put on the dreaded black cap.

Among many murder cases I covered were those of child-killer Raymond Morris, labelled The Monster Of Cannock Chase', and the notorious 'Black Panther' Donald Neilson who shot dead three men during post office robberies and also kidnapped and murdered teenager Lesley Whittle.

Throughout the 1970s and 1980s, I continued writing about crime from time to time though my career was moving increasingly into show-business journalism. Even so, in 1991 murder crossed my path again – this time very personally when a friend was brutally killed.

Brian Shearer was an antiques dealer I had known some years. He was a specialist in oak furniture, had a shop in Leek, North Staffordshire and was a familiar face around local antiques auctions. He bought fine oak furniture in the Midlands and took the best pieces down to London to sell to other dealers or private clients.

I have a keen interest in antiques – I have written three books on the subject – and over the years bought items from Brian and sometimes sold him items I had come across. Brian was an eccentric character who had a fiery temper if crossed but could be kind and generous.

By 1990, we had both moved to different parts of the country and were seldom in touch, so it was a shock when I read in the newspapers that Brian, then 69, had been found strangled and robbed in his house in Northamptonshire. Having once been features editor on the daily newspaper in Northampton, the Chronicle & Echo, I still had contacts there and rang the news editor to say I knew the victim. I gave an over-the-phone interview and the paper ran a front-page news story. Soon after, I received a telephone call at my home in Staffordshire from the police, asking if two Scotland Yard detectives could visit me as I might be able to help them with background details about Brian. He lived alone, had no relatives and it seemed they knew little about his private life.

I sat down with the two detectives and told them all I knew about Brian including the fact that he regularly used the M6 and M1 motorways to take furniture to London. The officers asked me if he was likely to stop and pick up hitch-hikers and I told them that he certainly would – he was an ex-Barnardo's boy and would always stop to pick up male hitch-hikers, often taking them home where he would cook them a meal and give them money to help them on their way.

Soon after, two young men were arrested and charged with Brian's murder, convicted and given life sentences. Described in court as 'drifters', the men were thumbing a lift near a motorway and Brian had picked them up and taken them to his home. There, they had killed and robbed him.

Of course, many murders are not so straightforward to unravel and even when killers are caught, the eventual outcome can sometimes be surprising or even shocking, as the cases I have selected for this book clearly illustrate.

Cases featured include:

A man who was tried for murder but acquitted, yet later the same day confessed he was the killer, knowing he could not be tried twice for the same crime.

A killer who cheated the hangman not once but three times and then went on to tour theatres, making a good living explaining how he did it.

A murder trial so sensitive, it was conducted in secret on a ship anchored off the Kent coast and the verdict never officially disclosed.

A case where even the prosecuting barrister told the judge that the man in the dock on a triple-murder charge was almost certainly not guilty and should not be convicted.

A murder victim said to frequently return to the scene of the crime hoping to meet her lover - the man who killed her.

ACKNOWLEDGEMENTS

Research for this book has involved multiple sources including contemporary newspaper reports and subsequent published accounts in magazines and books, Press archives and internet sites too numerous to mention, along with my own crime files and personal research and location visits.

However, I must single out the excellent book Bodies And Crime – A Pathologist Speaks by the eminent pathologist Denis Hocking (The Book Guild ,1992) as a source of information relating to a confusing and contradictory murder at the Housel Bay Hotel in Cornwall in 1943. Dr Hocking, the Cornwall County Pathologist at the time of the murder, examined the body of the victim and gave crucial evidence at the trial. He was also able to chronicle some remarkable events which occurred at the murder scene long after the crime was committed.

Another book, The Man They Couldn't Hang by Mike Holgate and Ian David Waugh (Sutton Publishing, 2005) deserves mention not only for its remarkably detailed account of the case of John Lee, but also for the authors' tireless research into what eventually happened to him.

Also notable is the book Perfect Murder by Bernard Taylor and Stephen Knight (Grafton, 1987) in which the aftermath of the Brighton Trunk Murder is one of several vintage murders compellingly detailed.

I am also grateful for information from the Kent and Essex Police Museums, the National Archives and former British Transport Police Officer Kevin Gordon.

My thanks to my friends and fellow journalists Neil Bonner and Mark Slack for invaluable advice and suggestions during the writing process. Thanks also to Doctor Louise Bonner and Catherine Roth for their helpful and constructive comments.

My wife Cassie merits special recognition for allowing me unlimited hours of undisturbed writing time. My thanks and love to her.

Nick Fletcher
South Devon, 2021

Also by Nick Fletcher

Novels

The Long Sunset
Imperfect Day

Short Story Collections

Escaping The Rain
Dark Edges
Snapshot

Poetry

Lost Avenues
Dark Heart

www.nickfletcher.co.uk

A QUESTION OF MOTIVE

When a middle-aged housewife was found dead in woodland near her home and three gold rings torn from her fingers, it seemed clear that the motive for this brutal murder was robbery. It was thought that a stranger, possibly an itinerant or a local petty thief, had by chance encountered the woman at this remote location and took the opportunity to attack and rob her.

Yet police at the scene were quickly forced to doubt the probability of this promising line of enquiry. Firstly, the woman was wearing gloves so the rings on her fingers could not be seen, which suggested her assailant may have already known they were there. More significantly, police found that though the woman had initially been struck from behind and knocked to the ground, she had then been shot twice in the head.

This was an astonishing discovery because at the time of this crime in 1908, it was very uncommon in rural areas for thieves to carry guns, let alone use them, and if robbery was the motive, as the attacker had already knocked the woman to the ground and could take the rings without any resistance, why the need to shoot her?

The conclusion was that Mrs Caroline Luard, the wife of retired army Major-General Charles Luard may have been the victim of a well-planned murder committed by someone she knew.

What followed was a strange and often murky murder investigation with little hard evidence, strewn with false leads and hampered by local rumours, poison-pen letters and a tight-lipped community which eventually all combined to create another terrible tragedy.

Caroline Luard, 58, was murdered on August 24th 1908 near her home in the Kent village of Ightham. She and her husband Charles, who was 69, had been married for 33 years and were a popular couple in the village, often seen walking out together and attending social events. They had two sons, one who had died from fever during army service in Africa, the other still a serving soldier.

Charles Luard was a Justice Of The Peace, a County Councillor, a school governor, a close friend of the local MP and of the Chief Constable. He and his wife were well-respected and involved

1

themselves in village life, especially Mrs Luard who was involved in several local charities.

The murder of Mrs Luard shocked not only their village and the county of Kent but far beyond, and although initially police thought her killer was probably local, the search was extended nationwide.

However, little headway was made. There were few clues found at the crime scene and even those that were found were mis-interpreted. And some lines of investigation which should have been followed up at an early stage were delayed or disregarded because of the status of the Luards and their connections with local officialdom.

To put all that into context we need to look in more detail at just what happened on that fateful August afternoon when Caroline Luard was murdered.

Monday August 24th was a bright sunny day and just after lunch, General Luard told his wife he planned to walk to the golf club at nearby Godden Green to collect his clubs, and Caroline said she would walk part of the way with him and then return home as she was expecting a neighbour, Mrs Alice Stewart, for afternoon tea.

The Luards set off at around 2.30pm and after walking about three quarters of a mile, reached a bungalow-style summer house on land owned by their friend Horace Wilkinson and which was set in woodland and with a public footpath nearby. A few hundred yards past this summerhouse, Mrs Luard decided she had walked far enough and would return home in order to prepare for her friend coming for tea. General Luard carried on to the golf club and three witnesses were able to confirm they saw him at the club between 3.20 and 3.40pm. At just after 4pm, General Luard met the local vicar who was driving by and who offered him a lift home, dropping him and his golf clubs off at 4.25pm.

When General Luard arrived at his house, he saw Mrs Stewart waiting there and she told him there was no sign of his wife. The General made Mrs Stewart some tea and after a few minutes said he could not understand why his wife was not there and he must go look for her.

He set off on the route they had taken earlier in the day as it was the route he knew she would use to return home. When he reached the summerhouse, he found his wife on the veranda, lying on the concrete floor, her face and head covered in blood. She was cold and dead. He noticed that one of her gloves lay nearby and that the three rings she wore on her left hand were missing. Examining her more closely he saw she had been shot in the head.

The General ran three hundred yards to the nearest house - that of his friend Horace Wilkinson - and raised the alarm. The first person he saw was the Wilkinson's coachman who recalling the incident later said: 'The General was breathing heavily – it was obvious he had been running hard. He was greatly agitated and couldn't speak. I told him to get his breath and then he gasped: 'Dead. Shot.'

The coachman then fetched the Wilkinson's butler who later described the General as 'frenzied with grief' and barely able to speak. All he could say between sobbing was: 'My wife is dead.'

The butler and the coachman took General Luard back to the summerhouse where Caroline Luard lay prone. The general was shouting: 'The brutes, they've killed her' and he knelt beside the body sobbing.

The local police constable was called and he immediately sent for senior officers from Sevenoaks. By the time they arrived, accompanied by a doctor, it was around 7.45 pm and getting dark. It was too late for any crime scene investigation so the body of Mrs Luard was removed and police officers were left to guard the location.

Next morning, a murder investigation swung into action and enquiries quickly established the time of the murder. Two independent witnesses at different locations who were within earshot of the summerhouse both said they heard shots at 3.15pm. At this crucial time, three other witnesses saw General Luard at his golf club almost a mile away from the murder scene. So the hunt was now on for someone else, probably a stranger using the footpath or walking through the woods, or perhaps a poacher or a hop-picker of which there were many in the area.

Apart from some inconclusive footprints heading away from the summerhouse towards the main road, there was little to go on so the local police, after 48 hours of getting nowhere, called in Scotland Yard who sent an inspector and a sergeant to take control of the investigation.

They arrived just in time for the opening of the inquest into Caroline

Luard's death, and the first witness was General Luard who sat with his head bowed. After answering a few questions about his movements on the day of the murder and his finding the body of his wife, the General was asked if he owned any revolvers. He confirmed he owned several but when asked if he had any ammunition for them, he said he had, but couldn't remember where he kept it.

A gun expert who later examined the revolvers said they could not have been used in the shooting of Mrs Luard as they were a smaller calibre than the gun used in the murder. It is worth noting that at that time - 1908 - gun ownership was less regulated and revolvers and rifles were not uncommon in many local communities, especially in rural areas. Gun ownership was much more tightly regulated after a new Firearms Act was introduced in 1920.

At the inquest the General was also asked if he knew anyone who might have had a grudge against him or his wife. 'None whatever.' he said. There had been speculation that someone from his military past may have had a reason to seek revenge or retribution but there was no evidence at all to support this theory and also, many years had elapsed since the General had left the military. Three witnesses confirmed their sightings of the General and the times he was seen, and other witnesses confirmed that the time they heard the shots was 3.15 pm.

A doctor who carried out the post-mortem said there were two bullet wounds, one behind Mrs Luard's right ear and one on the left temple with scorch marks suggesting they were fired at close range. He also found a wound to the back of head which he suggested was the result of a blow from a blunt instrument. He said that in his opinion, Mrs Luard was struck from behind, knocked to the floor and then shot twice.

The inquest was adjourned while police enquiries continued. Bloodhounds were used to search the area around the summerhouse but the results were inconclusive, especially as since the body was found, many police officers had tramped around. A ring similar to one stolen from Mrs Luard turned up in Tonbridge a few days later but later examination ruled it out, and a scrap of torn paper found near the scene turned out to be just a list of village names dropped by a hiker or cyclist.

A few days later, the funeral of Caroline Luard was held and the General attended, 'looking sorrowful' according to a reporter who was there, and as the coffin was lowered, the General tossed a bunch of

4

daisies onto it – Daisy was a pet-name for his wife.

Police inquiries continued, a wide area around the summerhouse was cleared, a nearby pond was dragged and a Press theory about a tramp committing the crime was dismissed as tramps were not usually armed with guns.

However, there was a shock when the Scotland Yard detective overseeing the case gave a Press interview. In it he said:' In the opinion of the police, the crime was carefully planned and not an inspiration of the moment. The market value of the rings which were stolen was insufficient to justify murder so there was clearly another motive.'

However, he had no idea what that motive could be.

The murder had attracted tremendous publicity given the high-status of the victim and her husband and the mystery surrounding the motive. Newspaper readers started writing in with their own bizarre theories, a clairvoyant sent in a detailed description of the murderer and various hoax claims were made including letters sent purporting to be from the murderer.

Meantime, the adjourned inquest was resumed. The General said neither he nor his wife had ever received any threatening letters nor knew of anyone who might bear them a grudge. Various witnesses came and went, confirming times and places, and despite no new information coming
light, police were granted a further adjournment while their enquiries continued.

Since the day of the murder, General Luard had been staying with various friends as he did not want to be alone in his own house. He quickly decided he did not want to live there again and arranged for the lease to be sold and the furniture and contents cleared. He was also upset by a number of anonymous letters he had received accusing him of his wife's murder, and he was aware of similar murmurings within the village itself.

The General was waiting for the return from South Africa of his son Charles, a captain in the Norfolk Regiment. His ship was due to dock at Southampton on Saturday September 19th and the General intended to travel there to meet him.

The day before the General was due to go to Southampton, he stayed at Barham Court in Maidstone, home of his friend Colonel Charles Warde, the local MP and brother of the Chief Constable of Kent. Over conversation at dinner, the General said he had asked the coroner to excuse him from attending the resumption of the adjourned inquest but that the coroner had insisted he be there in case any new evidence was produced.

At length the two men retired to bed and next morning, the butler took the General some tea and not long after, a maid saw the General going out for a stroll before breakfast, as he often did when staying at the house.

What happened next had a seismic effect on the case – General Luard walked along a footpath to the South Eastern and Chatham railway line and threw himself under a train, dying instantly.

In his pocket was a note which said: 'Please take my body to Barham Court'.

There in his bedroom, the General had left several letters, and in one he wrote: 'I am sick of the scandalous and lying reports, and I cannot face my son.'

In another letter, addressed to Colonel Warde, he wrote:

My dear Warde
I am sorry to have to return your kindness and hospitality and long friendship in this way but I am satisfied that it is best to join her in the second life at once, as I can be of no further use to anyone in the future in this world, of which I am tired and in which I do not wish to live any longer.
I thought that my strength was sufficient to bear up against the horrible imputation and the terrible letters which I have received since that awful crime was committed which robbed me of my happiness. The goodness, kindness and sympathy of so many friends has kept me going. But somehow, now in the last day or two, something seems to have snapped. The strength has left me and I care for nothing except to join her again.
So goodbye, dear friend, to both of us.
Yours very affectionately,
C.E. Luard

PS I shall be somewhere on the line of railway.

You may think that such a terrible tragedy would draw a line under this mysterious murder case, but far from it. In a way, there was a new beginning for both locally and nationally there was still intense speculation about who killed Caroline Luard, and more significantly - why.

Any hope that public interest would fade away after the conclusion of the inquest was dashed, despite coroner Thomas Buss doing his best to curtail it.

At the inquest, he said: 'The matter of Mrs Luard's death is still under investigation, but even now I think it my duty to make some kind of reference to the many reports – the many base insinuations I will call them– in the shape of anonymous letters which have been sent to General Luard, suggesting almost that he was responsible for the death of his wife. These letters are innumerable. They have also been received by the police and by myself in numbers. I was disgusted when I heard of such suggestions. And I will say this - those persons who have been prompted to write these letters, instead of sympathizing with General Luard in the great trouble he had undergone, added to the poignancy of his grief; and since the death of his wife, I imagine that to the sensitive and honourable man that he was, they made his life almost unbearable.

'That, no doubt, was a great factor in inducing him to rid himself of his present life, and if those writers have any conscience at all they will reflect, and feel at any rate that they must have contributed more or less to the doom to which the General sent himself. Let us hope that although they treated him so badly in the last remaining days of his life, they will respect his memory now and utter no more of these baseless and unfounded insinuations.'

This was extremely strong stuff from a coroner, but he hadn't quite finished. He then directly addressed the question of General Luard being involved in the death of his wife, saying evidence from 'half a dozen witnesses' had confirmed the General's movements on the day of the murder. 'I need hardly say that he could not have been present and committed this terrible act,' he said.

The jury agreed. They bought in a verdict of 'wilful murder by some person or persons unknown'.

Speculation about the murder continued, fanned by continued and often sensationalist Press coverage which was further amplified by the

7

General's friend Colonel Warde offering a £1,000 reward (about £120,000 in today's money) for information leading to an arrest and conviction. More letters poured in making various fanciful claims but no new evidence was found.

A year later, a sensational breakthrough hit the headlines – a man was arrested and charged with the murder of Mrs Luard. The man was David Woodruff, an elderly tramp who when previously arrested a few months earlier had been carrying a revolver. This information had inexplicably only just come to the attention of detectives dealing with the Luard case. Woodruff denied ever having visited the village of Ightham but was arrested and charged with murder and rushed to Maidstone court where in a farcical development, he was quickly released from custody and sent on his way when the red-faced police were forced to admit they had overlooked one crucial fact – at the time of Mrs Luard's murder, Woodruff had a cast-iron alibi – he was actually behind bars in Maidstone prison serving a four-month sentence.

The case then faded away from the headlines though crime journalists and authors have over the years presented a variety of theories of their own. Some think robbery was not the real motive for killing Mrs Luard as it would have been easier to have just knocked her down, snatched the rings and run away, which was initially what appeared to have happened. But Mrs Luard was also shot twice in the head. The most obvious theory is revenge for something that she or her husband had done in their past.

That is of course possible but the decision for the Luards to take a walk that morning was spur of the moment, it was not a regular habit of theirs, so how could someone seeking revenge know they were going along that secluded woodland path that day?

Researchers have also closely scrutinized the Luard's relationship and their past activities but no reason for revenge has surfaced.

Another suggestion was that Mrs Luard was killed by a man called John Dickman, who in 1910, two years after the Luard murder, was convicted of shooting dead and robbing a man on a train, and was hung. The alleged connection to Mrs Luard was flimsy at best. It was suggested that when arrested, Dickman had on him a cheque for £10 from Mrs Luard and dated 1908, two years earlier, which she had sent to him after seeing a newspaper advertisement that he was a gentleman who needed financial help. This dubious claim stems from a brief reference from a judge, made not in court but in a private letter to a journalist in reply to an enquiry about Dickman's conviction. Leaving aside the question of why a murderer would for two years carry with him a cheque linking him to a previous murder, there was no reference to such a letter at Dickman's trial, and it certainly would have been mentioned given such a sensational claim. There is no evidence at all that Mrs Luard responded to a newspaper advertisement, or sent a cheque to Dickman.

There is one other theory which has been offered which is in some ways more plausible, though still unlikely. That the killer was the General himself. After all, he was definitely near the scene of the crime and had the opportunity.

The time of the murder was fixed only by the sound of gunshots. But if the General had killed his wife even half an hour earlier at the summerhouse and somehow managed to muffle the sound of the shots, he could then have fired two further shots at around 3.15pm when he was nearer to the golf club, knowing he would he would then have witnesses to him being there. He would also have taken the rings from his wife's hand to suggest robbery was the motive for the attack.

The General had admitted owning several revolvers which had been examined and eliminated because they were the wrong calibre, but he could of course have had another smaller-calibre revolver hidden away. And it seemed suspicious that when asked to show police his ammunition, he said he couldn't remember where it was, perhaps because he knew some smaller-calibre bullets might be found.

Once the inquest was over, police were continuing their investigations and the General may have thought they might to turn their attention to him, questioning him about the revolvers, the missing ammunition, perhaps even searching the house and grounds.

That, and the fact he might be riddled with guilt over what he had done and had still to face his son who had just returned from abroad might have overwhelmed him, and rather than face the consequences he had chosen to take an exit route under the wheels of a train.

This scenario is plausible but, in my view, it falls down when it comes to motive. There just doesn't appear to be one. The couple had a wide circle of friends who all felt they were very happy together and though Caroline was 11 years younger than her husband, there was no suggestion she had any interest in another man, or that the couple had any issues over money or family matters. Nor were there any signs at all of the General having any mental or psychological problems that might have distorted his thinking.

Over a century later it is impossible to come to any solid conclusion as to who murdered Caroline Luard but my own instinctive feeling after reading many accounts of the case is that Mrs Luard almost certainly died at the hands of a chance thief who was just passing by and saw an easy opportunity to rob a lone woman in a remote location. While it was unlikely such a thief would be armed, it is quite possible – evidenced by the tramp James Woodruff who did carry a gun, and other instances that had occurred elsewhere involving petty thieves being armed.

Whoever killed Caroline Luard could have used a gun just to make absolutely certain there was no chance of ever being identified. Whoever it was, they certainly succeeded in that.

THE MAN ON THE ROOF

On a cool October evening in 1912, the lives of three people became fatefully connected in the Sussex seaside resort of Eastbourne. One was a Countess, one a police officer, the other a criminal. None of the three knew each other but all three were to become central characters in a sensational murder trial which not only shocked the nation but created international headlines.

This bizarre crime began around 7.15 pm on that October evening when wealthy Hungarian Countess Flora Sztaray, a local resident, set out to meet friends for dinner at the nearby Burlington Hotel, a grand Victorian building overlooking the seafront and pier. The Countess had booked a horse-drawn carriage to take her to the hotel and it arrived promptly outside her house in tree-lined South Cliff Avenue.

However, as soon as the carriage moved away from the house, the coachman told the Countess that on arrival he had seen the figure of a man crouched on the roof of the portico that sheltered the front door of the property. He had not wanted to alert her at the time as it may have put her in danger. The Countess immediately ordered the coachman to return and in a just a few minutes they were back at the house where she too could see a dark figure on the portico as they approached. Getting out of the carriage, she made sure the man on the roof heard her tell the coachman she had forgotten something and would be back shortly, but once inside she telephoned the police.

There was a police station on the nearby seafront parade and Inspector Arthur Walls, who was based there, quickly went to South Cliff Avenue and arrived at about 7.40pm. The crouched figure was still on the roof and Inspector Walls called to the man to come down. There was no reply and then two shots were fired, one of them killing Inspector Walls, a father of three children and a veteran with 24 years police service.

Several people in the vicinity heard the shots and came running to the scene. They found the police officer dead and no sign of the man who had been on the roof. Lying in the road nearby was a felt hat but whether it was connected to the crime was unknown.

The Chief Constable, Major Edward Teale, lived close by and quickly took charge of the investigation and immediately sought help from Scotland Yard, who sent two CID officers to Eastbourne on the overnight train, arriving in Eastbourne at 8.10am the next day.

But there was little to go on, just the felt hat and some footprints in the garden of the house which may or may not have been those of the killer.

Yet that evening, an extraordinary development took place. A young man called Edgar Power, a former medical student who described himself as a doctor, walked into Eastbourne Police Station and calmly informed officers that he knew who had murdered Inspector Walls.

Power told police the man who shot the police officer used several aliases but was now using the name John Williams. He said Williams had been staying at an address in Tideswell Road, Eastbourne, with his pregnant girlfriend Florence Seymour but he had fled to London that day on the afternoon train.

Power refused to make an official statement as he said he wanted his name kept out of the matter, but he said his information was reliable because he knew John Williams and Williams had admitted to him that he had shot the police officer. According to Power, Williams had met his girlfriend after the shooting and the two had agreed to bury the revolver on the beach.

The police had some doubt about the total veracity of Power's story. Apart from passing himself off as a doctor despite not being qualified, he also had two minor previous convictions himself. But the police had no other leads to follow and as Power said he had to go to London later that day they let him go pending further enquiries.

Two days later, Power telephoned the police and told them he had set a trap by arranging to meet the murder suspect John Williams at Moorgate Street railway station in London so the police could arrest him. The police surrounded the station cafe and when Williams turned up, they arrested him and also the informant Edgar Power.

Both men were questioned and a complex situation came to light. The reason Power had been keen to help police was because he was in love with Williams' girlfriend Florence Seymour who was described as a girl of 'remarkable beauty'.

Police brought in Florence for questioning and while she denied knowing anything about the murder of Inspector Walls, she did admit

Williams had lost a soft hat on the night of murder. While at the police station, Florence was seen trying to throw a piece of paper onto an open fire and when retrieved the paper was a left-luggage ticket for Victoria Station. Police went there and found a Gladstone bag containing a leather belt with a revolver holster attached. But there was no gun.

While Williams was in custody, Power and Florence Seymour – who was heavily pregnant and in poor health – left London and returned to Eastbourne. Power persuaded the girl to reveal just where on the beach she and Williams had buried the gun, saying that if the police found it, it would help convict Williams of murder. He told her they should go and retrieve it and take it to a safer place and she agreed. But in a callous act of betrayal of the woman he loved, Power then tipped off the police who kept them under surveillance and arrested Florence when the gun was found.

During her interview with detectives, Florence admitted that while she had not been with Williams at the time of the murder, she had met him soon afterwards and went with him while he buried gun. She said Williams told her he hadn't shot the police officer but he did have a gun so didn't want to be caught with it because of his criminal record.

The gun was given to the noted forensics expert Robert Churchill for examination and his findings would prove to be controversial.

At a glance, the case against John Williams looked solid and his long police record helped underpin it. Williams was born in Edinburgh in 1883 and his real name was George McKay but he stopped using the name when he turned to crime, supposedly to protect his father who was a clergyman.

At the time he was charged with the murder of Inspector Arthur Walls, Williams was 29 years old and had been a criminal since the age of 9 when he began petty thieving. Over the following 20 years, Williams became a career criminal using at least a dozen different names. Even when he went into the army in 1899, serving in the Scots Guards Regiment and posted to South Africa, he robbed the regimental stores and was jailed for three months. He later deserted and joined the Rhodesian Horse Regiment where he was soon court-martialled for stealing money and sentenced to two years hard labour. In 1906 he was deported from South Africa as 'an undesirable'.

Back in England, he had continued to steal, and racked up several convictions and prison terms for fraud, burglary and housebreaking which ended when he was arrested and charged with the murder of Inspector Walls. While initially the case against Williams appeared very solid it was mostly circumstantial and the case was to become even more clouded by subsequent developments including the chief prosecution witness Florence Seymour retracting her police statement, saying it had been made under duress, and in another twist, someone else being named as the murderer!

These elements resulted in a trial described in the newspapers as 'the most sensational in living history' and which was to lead to the direct involvement of the Home Secretary.

A pre-trial hearing took place at Eastbourne Magistrates Court where Williams pleaded not guilty and told the magistrates: 'I would not a commit a crime like that.'

It had been decided that Florence Seymour, described as 'fragile and pale-faced', would give evidence first as it was felt there was a risk that she might retract her statement and that she was also in very poor health. During her evidence, she collapsed several times but did confirm her police statement and so Williams was committed for trial at Lewes Assizes.

The trial began on December 12th 1912 before Judge Arthur Channell, and Williams was represented by counsel Patrick Hastings who although only 32, was already noted for his skill in cross-examination and who would go on to become Attorney General in 1924. The Crown was represented by Sir Frederick Low.

Again, Florence Seymour was first in the witness box. She immediately retracted her previous statement, saying she made it after being pressured by Edgar Power who had told her that if she did not make the statement, she might herself be charged with murder. She also claimed police had threatened her and forced her to make the statement. This was a setback as prosecutor Sir Frederick Low had already told the court his case rested heavily on Seymour's testimony. He immediately asked the judge to allow him to treat Florence as an unwilling 'hostile' witness. The request was granted, but despite Low's persistent questioning, Florence would not admit anything that would incriminate Williams.

Edgar Power was next in the witness box and claimed he had seen

Williams with a gun and that Williams had confessed to him that he had killed Inspector Walls. In cross examination, Williams' counsel Patrick Hasting emphasised Power's lack of credibility and highlighted his callous betrayal of both his friend Williams, and Florence Seymour who he had professed to love. In a book published some years later Patrick Hastings described Edgar Power as 'the most utterly contemptible human being I have ever met.'

John Williams then gave evidence. He admitted he had a gun, which he said he had bought some nine months earlier from a man in London for two shillings, but the hammer was missing so it could not be fired. Williams admitted he and Florence were in the vicinity of the house of Countess Sztaray on the evening of the murder, but denied he was the man on the roof. He also said that he and Florence hid the gun because he had a criminal record of burglary and if arrested, didn't want to found in possession of a gun.

At this stage of the trial, even the prosecution was aware that chances of a conviction were slim as there was no solid evidence to link Williams to the crime, so they had to rely on what at that time was a new science, that of ballistics.

Although only 25, Robert Churchill was already regarded as a leading expert on the technique of matching bullet markings to the gun that fired them. The gun found buried on the beach had the hammer missing so Churchill had to fit a new one for test firing to get a bullet to compare with that which killed Inspector Walls. However, while Churchill could establish that the gun used to shoot Walls and the gun which Williams admitted having buried were of the same type and calibre, he could not get sufficiently clear photos of the internal marking of the barrel to say beyond doubt that the fatal bullet was fired from Williams' gun.

However, Churchill came up with an unusual method of trying to obtain such evidence – he decided that if he poured dental wax into the gun barrel, he could get an impression of the internal markings. This rather primitive method had never previously been used but Churchill managed to get what he regarded as a clear impression which he thought would prove the bullet that killed the police officer came from the gun in Williams' possession. This method was controversial at the time and almost certainly would not have been acceptable evidence in a modern court.

Yet Churchill was adamant the markings were identical and was prepared to give evidence on that point at the trial. The fate of John Williams rested on Churchill being able to convince a jury.

And he did. In a case where convincing evidence was in short supply, the jury were swayed by Churchill's ballistics evidence – they were out for just 15 minutes before finding Williams guilty of murder, and he was sentenced to be hanged.

Defence counsel Patrick Hasting immediately lodged an appeal and it was heard a month later. Hasting argued that the judge had misdirected the jury but the appeal court chairman Lord Alverstone rejected the appeal.

Writing of the case some years later, Patrick Hasting said of Lord Alverstone: 'From the outset of the hearing it was apparent that he was satisfied with the prisoner's guilt and no legal argument seemed to make the least impression on him.'

Yet there was still another astonishing twist in this remarkable case – while in prison awaiting his execution date, John Williams received a letter from a criminal pal known as Freddie Mike, who said he knew the name of the real murderer – it was his own twin brother who had fled to France soon after the shooting of Inspector Walls!

Police went to see Freddie, who stood by the story and all the details were sent to the Home Secretary and were widely reported in the Press. Various campaigns began in an attempt to free John Williams and 35,000-signature petition was sent to the Home Secretary Reginald McKenna. There were also questions raised in the House Of Commons, with several MPs asking for Williams to be pardoned in view of the lack of direct evidence, the contradictory nature of the circumstances and the misdirection of the judge's summing up to the jury.

It was a short-lived hope for Williams, as further enquiries revealed that Freddie Mike's story was a complete fabrication. Freddie had no twin brother, and appeared to have invented the story in a bid to save his friend from the gallows.

Hopes of a pardon were also dashed as Home Secretary refused to intervene and Williams' execution date was set. Meantime Florence Seymour was due to give birth. The publicity in the case had made her a despised figure in Eastbourne and local hospitals refused to admit her to have the baby - she had to go by train to Hastings, 14 miles away, to have her child and her confinement was personally paid for by Williams' lawyer Patrick Hastings and his wife.

Williams twice applied for permission to marry Florence, he was desperate to legitimise the child, but permission was refused. However, the authorities did allow Florence to take the child into prison for Williams to see it. He held the baby and kissed it, and then pressed a tiny piece of bread into the baby's hand and said: 'Now at least you can't say your father never gave you anything.'
On January 29th 1913 John Williams was hung. He made no last-minute confession to the murder.

What became of Florence and her baby is not known. She certainly left Eastbourne but wherever her destination may have been, I feel it is most unlikely she had any more to do with Edgar Power, the man who was obsessed with her, yet had cruelly betrayed her and sent her lover John Williams to the gallows. Power also vanished. Publicly reviled and condemned, it is believed he fled abroad.

Should John Williams have been convicted of murder? I do not think so, and my view is shared by his counsel Patrick Hastings who almost 20 years after the trial said: 'To this day I am satisfied he should not have been hanged. The anxiety which haunted me throughout that sordid trial remains with me.'

John Williams was never identified as being seen at the murder location, the hat found at the scene could not be traced to him, nor the footprints in the garden. His criminal record showed he did not normally carry a gun, nor was there any reason for him to shoot Inspector Walls – Williams was an experienced criminal and would have known that if caught, the worst he would face was a charge of attempted house-breaking which would carry a relatively light sentence, despite his record. He would have known too that the penalty for shooting a police officer was hanging.

Also, the ballistics evidence was far from conclusive, even though the jury accepted it. A wax impression of microscopic marking on the inside of a gun barrel would not by modern standards have been sufficiently accurate to prove beyond reasonable doubt that the gun had fired the fatal bullet.

I also feel that the evidence given by Edgar Power was tainted. He was motivated by his desire for Florence Seymour and wanted

Williams out of the way so he could be with her. We have only his word that Williams confessed to the crime - the word of a man who was a fraud, who was posing as a doctor, who had criminal convictions himself and was described in one report as being 'a man of notoriously bad character'.

The final summing up by Judge Channell was crucial, yet it seemed less than impartial. He told the jury that hiding the gun and then fleeing to London were 'the acts of a guilty man'. And while he said there was 'no direct evidence' to link John Williams to the crime, he then told the jury that they could take into account Florence Seymour's original statement – even though she claimed it was made under duress and which she later fully retracted. Without that statement, there was no hard evidence against John Williams.

However, while I think that Williams should not have been convicted on the evidence before the court, that does not necessarily mean he was innocent. He was in the vicinity of the murder at the time, he did have a long history of house-breaking and theft, and he did have a gun his possession. The chances of another armed burglar being on the roof of the home of Countess Szstaray at precisely that time is very remote.

Williams probably killed Inspector Walls in a moment of panic or perhaps when firing what he thought was a warning shot which in the darkness hit the police inspector by chance. But 'probably' is not good enough for a conviction, let alone a hanging. In Britain, then as now, guilt must be beyond all reasonable doubt. In my opinion, in the case of John Williams it was not.

THE FARMHOUSE MURDERS

It was clear that a truly extraordinary event must have occurred when a prosecuting barrister whose job it is to get a conviction, opens the case against a man charged with three murders by telling the court that it was 'almost inconceivable' that the man in the dock could have committed the crimes.

The event that led to that dramatic statement began five months earlier in the quiet village of West Charleton near Kingsbridge in Devon. On the edge of the village was Croft Farm, a property owned and farmed by 71-year-old Thomas Maye and his wife Emily,70. Also living with them were two of their daughters, Joan and Gwyneth who were in their late twenties, and their handyman and gardener Charles Lockhart, who was 22.

It was Lockhart who made the shocking discovery that was to result in a bizarre murder trial that gained sensational news coverage and sparked gossip and speculation across the county and far beyond.

On Thursday June 11th 1936, Lockhart went to a dance in Stokenham, a neighbouring village some three miles from West Charleton, spent the evening there with various friends and acquaintances and returned to Croft Farm around 2.45am. When he opened the door and went into the farmhouse, he came across an horrific scene. The body of the Maye's daughter Gwyneth was lying in a pool of blood in the hallway. She was unconscious but still alive and had severe head injuries.

Despite knowing that Gwyneth's parents and sister should also be in the house, Lockhart rather inexplicably ran from the building to fetch the village constable William Mugridge. It is probable that Lockhart felt his first priority was to get help for the injured Gwyneth, or he may have just panicked, but whatever his reason he alerted the constable and also raised another farmworker Frank Lee and together the three men went back to the scene, little knowing that much worse was still to come.

As they entered the farmhouse they encountered a strong smell of paraffin and saw that carpets and curtains in parts of the house were ablaze and they used buckets of water to put out the flames before fully searching the property. Upstairs they discovered Gwyneth's sister Joan lying outside her bedroom door, dead from a fractured skull.

Then they went into the bedroom of her parents and found her father Thomas sprawled on a bed which was still burning. He had three deep wounds to his forehead and an injury to his jaw, but was semi-conscious and asked constable Mugridge: 'Where has my wife gone?'

Mugridge knew the answer to that question – he could see that Emily Maye was on the floor beside the bed, out of sight of her husband, dead from a fractured skull and her body partly burned.

Constable Mugridge seemed to find it difficult to grasp the situation, perhaps not surprising as village bobbies are rarely confronted with vicious murders, and he then made a significant error for which he was later to be reprimanded.

It appears Mugridge immediately took the view that as the three women were dead and Thomas Maye was still alive, he must have been the assailant perhaps because of some family argument that had taken place. Thomas Maye was still lying on the bed, and in dazed and confused. He asked the policeman why he was in the bedroom, Mugridge told him: 'Your wife sent for me as the house was on fire.' It was an extraordinary remark given Mugridge already knew Mrs Maye was dead.

Mugridge was clearly out of his depth and then made a procedural error by failing to caution Maye before asking: 'What have you done?' which was later viewed as an accusation or murder.

While they waited for a doctor to arrive, the murder scenes were checked and a walling hammer – an implement which had both a hammer head and an axe blade - was found next to Gwyneth's body in the hallway. Part of the handle was missing and was found upstairs next to the body of Joan. It appeared that the killer had first attacked Mrs Maye in the bedroom, and then her daughters as they perhaps heard noises and went to investigate. The implication was the attacker was Mr Maye, who had then inflicted his own wounds to suggest he too was attacked by an intruder.

When the doctor arrived, he found Gwyneth barely alive and had her rushed to the nearby Kingsbridge Cottage Hospital where she died some four hours later without ever regaining consciousness.

The doctor then turned his attention to Thomas Maye who was now able to stand up and get dressed. Maye had three deep cuts to his head, each one causing a skull fracture. The doctor was convinced the head wounds had been caused by the same hammer which had been used on the three women and that the blows were severe enough to have immediately rendered Maye unconscious. The doctor was certain they could not have been self-inflicted.

Told he should be taken to hospital, Maye initially refused and was therefore present when a police inspector arrived. The house had now been thoroughly searched and there was no evidence of a break in, nor of an intruder, and no sign of theft either, despite there being money, jewellery and other valuables in the property. The inspector asked Maye to explain what had happened and Maye gave a clear account of the evening – the family had supper together, then the two daughters went to bed early. At 9.30 pm Maye said he was going to bed and his wife Emily said she would join him as soon as she had finished some sewing. He said he kissed his wife goodnight and went to bed, and had no memory whatsoever of anything that happened after that.

Thomas Maye seemed open and frank with the police but it became clear his health was fast deteriorating and he was taken to Kingsbridge Infirmary for treatment and later moved to a nursing home in Plymouth where he spent several weeks recovering. During that period, he often asked why his wife and daughters hadn't visited, as if unaware they were dead.

The only other suspect, the handyman Charles Lockhart had been quickly eliminated as there were a number of witnesses who confirmed he had been at the dance in Stokenham at the time the murders took place. So it was no surprise that on July 15th Maye was told he would be charged with the three murders. He described the move as 'absurd', adding: 'I loved my wife and daughters too well.'

Two weeks passed before Maye was brought before the court in Kingsbridge to be formally charged and it was clear that the prosecuting counsel Geoffrey Roberts was somewhat perplexed at the lack of convincing evidence against Maye, who he described as a man of exemplary character with a happy domestic life. He could put forward no motive for the murders, and no reason for Maye to slaughter three of his family unless he had suffered some temporary mental breakdown. Mr Roberts said it 'almost inconceivable' Maye could have committed the crimes.

Defending counsel Mr F.S.Laskey produced the doctor who attended to Maye on the night of the murders and the doctor confirmed that the injuries to Maye's head were so severe, he would have almost immediately become unconscious and that the angle of the blows was such that they could not have been self-inflicted and appeared to be been struck while Mayes was lying in bed.

Giving evidence himself, Maye told the court that he loved his family, had no enemies, had no financial problems, and did not own and had never seen the murder weapon. He said he had no idea what happened that night, that his memory was totally blank from 9.30 pm when he went to bed.

His lawyer then submitted that in view of the lack of evidence, there was no case to answer and that the charges against Thomas Maye should be dropped.

However, that was not the end of this remarkable case - it was a new beginning. The local magistrates felt that despite the absence of any clear evidence in the case – which had attracted national publicity – the matter was too important for them to deal with. After a short adjournment for discussion, they returned to announce they were referring the case to a higher court.

A few months later in November, Maye stood in the dock at Devon Assizes charged with three murders. His face was still showing the scars of his own injuries.

Again Mr Geoffrey Roberts was prosecuting and he told the judge, Mr Justice Charles, that Mrs Emily Maye and her daughters Gwyneth and Joan were certainly murdered by the same person. But then, in an extraordinary move which astounded many of those in court, Mr Roberts declared that the prosecution was not going to seek a conviction and had no intention of trying to convince the jury that Thomas Maye was guilty. Mr Roberts said his duty was to just place the facts before the court.

It was a sensational development and the implication was clear – even the prosecution thought Thomas Maye was innocent.

Various witnesses were called to testify to Maye's good character and two men – an accountant and a farrier – who had visited Mr Maye at the farmhouse around 7pm on the evening the murders both told the court they found everything normal. They described Maye as 'a kindly man' who seemed 'on affectionate terms' with his family.

Among the witnesses was Constable William Mugridge and Maye's defence counsel F.S Laskey immediately took him to task over his accusatory manner in asking Maye: 'What have you done?' when he found him barely conscious in the bedroom. 'Without any evidence whatsoever, you made up your mind he was guilty of murdering his wife and daughters,' Laskey told him.

Mugridge was also rebuked by the judge for jumping to a conclusion 'which may have been entirely wrong.'

The doctor was called to the witness box and again confirmed that he was certain Maye could not have inflicted his own wounds, and that bruising to his jaw suggested he has been punched before being struck with the hammer.

Mr Justice Charles had heard enough. He directed the jury to find Thomas Maye not guilty of the murder of his wife and two daughters. Summing up, the judge chose his words carefully but it appeared he was somewhat surprised the case had ever reached the Assizes. He said this was not the fault of the prosecution, who were merely doing their job and who 'appeared to have called every witness who could have been of any assistance to the defence.'

After the verdict, Thomas Maye made a short statement to the Press. 'Thank God that terrible time is over,' he told reporters. 'I knew I would be proved innocent.'

As the dust settled over the case, no convincing theories were put forward about who might have committed the murders on that fateful night, or why, though there were still some in the locality who thought it could only have been Thomas Maye.

Maye did not continue farming. The following year the stock and equipment at Croft Farm were sold and much of the land leased to another farmer, while Maye lived in retirement with other family members. He lived for another 20 years, dying aged 91 and was laid to rest with his wife and daughters in the graveyard at St Mary's Church, West Charleton, a beautiful country church with a view of the sea.

This was an extraordinary and seemingly motiveless multiple murder which remains unsolved. In my view, there only two possible scenarios to explain it.

One is that Thomas Maye did murder his wife and daughters and self-inflicted his own wounds to cover his crime, and did it well enough to deceive a doctor and investigating police officers. This is very unlikely as all accounts indicate the Maye family were very happy together, and for Maye to have judged how severely to inflict his own wounds so that he was badly injured but would survive is even more remote.

The other explanation is much more likely – the family was attacked by someone who had a grudge against Thomas Maye. Whoever that was – almost certainly a man - killed Maye's wife and two daughters, and then attacked Maye, perhaps leaving the house thinking May's injuries were enough to be fatal. Or the killer might have deliberately injured Maye just enough to frame him - make it look as though Maye had murdered his own family, and then injured himself, which was exactly what police had initially concluded.

Grudges are often secretive and can be caused for the most insignificant reasons, sometimes even just a simple misunderstanding or minor disagreement and of course, often by jealousy. They can be 'nursed' for sometimes years before triggered into action. I think somewhere in his past, Thomas Maye had done or said something, even perhaps unintentionally, that had upset or angered someone and that person had harboured a grudge. And weeks, months or even years later on a summer's night at a remote location, that person took a terrible revenge.

THE SECOND SHOT

Two gunshots were heard, and a man running from the scene told someone he had just killed his girlfriend. Nearby, a young woman was found dead from two gunshot wounds. To anyone investigating, it would appear to be as clear a case of murder as you could find. Yet it was anything but clear.

What happened on that cold wet morning at a remote location on the Cornish coast resulted in an extraordinary murder trial and an even more astonishing aftermath.

The murder took place in 1943 at the Housel Bay Hotel at Lizard Point in Cornwall which at that time had been requisitioned by the Royal Air Force for use as a radar plotting station. Among the personnel at the hotel was Corporal Joan Lewis, an attractive 27-year-old, and it was her body which was found in the early hours of October 16th, slumped on the floor of a summerhouse in the grounds of the hotel.

Seen running from the summerhouse was the base commander, Flying Officer William Croft, who on reaching the hotel immediately told duty officer Norman Page he had just killed Joan Lewis. Croft than rang another officer and was heard to say: 'I have shot Joan.'

Croft, who was 32 and married with two children, had been having an affair with Joan Lewis, which was a breach of military regulations. As a result, Joan was to be transferred to another base later that same day so the couple's secret rendezvous in the summer house was to be their last. So what had gone wrong?

Duty officer Page and a sergeant ran to the summerhouse and found the body of Joan Lewis on the floor in a pool of blood. She had a bullet wound in her chest and another in her head. On a table near the body lay a Webley service revolver. Examination revealed two shots had been fired from it.

Croft then told the officers to call the police, saying that he and Joan could not bear to be parted and had agreed on a suicide pact. He then came up with an extraordinary explanation, claiming that Joan had actually fired both shots.

He said Joan had picked up the revolver to shoot herself, and he was then supposed to take the gun and use it on himself. However, he claimed Joan's first shot into her chest was not fatal and she said she was in great pain and asked him to get help. As he ran from the summer house, he heard a second shot, went back and found Joan had shot herself again, this time in the head.

Croft said he then picked up the revolver and tried to shoot himself, but the gun didn't fire, so he ran to the hotel to report the matter. It was a bizarre and incredible story that was to be at the centre of a sensational murder trial just a few weeks later.

Soon after the shooting, the Cornwall County Pathologist Dr Denis Hocking was on the scene, a very experienced and highly respected man noted for his meticulous methods. Hocking quickly established that the first shot was fired into the area of Joan's heart from a distance of about six inches. This did not rule out suicide, though in Hocking's experience, those attempting to commit suicide with a revolver tended to have the barrel pressed against them, not several inches away. He thought it 'unlikely' Joan shot herself.

What was very significant was Hocking's discovery that that first bullet had struck a rib and deflected, thus completely missing the girl's heart. It had exited underneath her armpit and had not immediately killed her.

The second shot presented its own mystery. It had penetrated Joan's forehead at a slight downward angle, suggesting it has been fired from above while she was sitting down on a small sofa in the summerhouse – a blood stain and the spent bullet were found on the back of the sofa.

There was no burning of the skin around the entry point on Joan's forehead and the spread pattern of unburned powder allowed Hocking to conclude the gun had been fired from a distance of at least eighteen inches - this meant it would not have been possible for Joan to have fired the gun herself.

He explained that the first shot, in exiting Joan's body, had severely damaged the chest muscles which would have been needed to help lift the heavy revolver to fire the second shot and that, coupled with trying to hold it away from her head at a distance of eighteen inches, meant it was impossible for her to get her finger on the trigger. She would have to have used her thumb, making the whole process impossible, especially as she was already badly injured from the first bullet. He added that even if she could have fired the second shot, the recoil would have forced her to drop the gun onto the floor - yet it was found on a table.

Hocking told the police he was adamant the girl had died from gunshot wounds 'inflicted by some other person.'

All the evidence pointed to William Croft having murdered Joan, and he was formerly charged. At a preliminary hearing on November 16th, 1943 at Helston Police Court, the prosecutor referred to letters exchanged between Croft and Joan Lewis. In one, Croft revealed that not only was he in love with Joan but that he was also very jealous and couldn't face them being parted. In one letter Croft said: 'The thought of you being in the company of another male drives me to distraction.'

At the hearing Croft denied killing Joan. 'She shot herself twice,' he said. 'We had both agreed to commit suicide.'

He said having decided on a suicide pact, they spent the night together in the summerhouse. They awoke about 4.30am and he placed his service revolver on his lap. He said they agreed that whoever felt like going first should pick up the gun and use it, the other one would then do the same. He claimed he then dozed off and was woken by the sound of a gunshot and saw Joan clasping her chest and begging him to get help. He ran towards the hotel but almost immediately heard a second shot and turned back to find Joan had shot herself in the head. He told the court his first instinct at that point was to complete the suicide pact by shooting himself, but when he picked up the gun and held it to his head and pulled the trigger, the gun failed to fire. It was then that he ran to the hotel to raise the alarm. It was an account which stretched credulity to its limits though it did explain why the gun was found on a table instead of on the floor.

Four weeks later on December 14th at Winchester Assizes, Croft stood in the dock charged with murder and a trial began which was to severely test Croft's suicide pact story and in due course provide further surprising twists.

Prosecuting counsel Mr John Maude convincingly laid out the case against Croft, calling Dr Hocking as his chief witness. Dr Hocking gave his forensic findings and also put himself through various contortions to demonstrate to the jury his assertion that while it was just about possible - though most unlikely – that Joan Lewis could have fired the first shot, it was impossible for her to have fired the second.

He said that if she had fired the first shot, she would have to have held the gun in a position so awkward that the recoil would have spun it out of her grasp and that it was 'beyond belief' that a badly injured woman in great pain would then crawl around on her hands and knees in the darkness trying to locate the gun in order to fire a second shot.

Defence counsel Humphrey Edmunds maintained that the death of Joan Lewis was due to a suicide pact that did not have its intended outcome, and he called Croft into the witness box.

Croft confirmed he and Joan were having a passionate affair and that they were both very unhappy about the order from their superiors that they were to be forcibly separated in order to break the romance.

He said on what was to be their final night together in the summerhouse – Joan was being transferred to a base in Devon the next day - he took his service revolver with him and they discussed suicide either by jumping off the cliffs or shooting each other. He had placed his revolver on his lap and they sat together, both 'highly strung' and scared about what they planned to do.

'We sat for some considerable time,' he told the court. 'I felt Joan's hand in mine and then I felt the weight of the revolver taken off my knee.'

It was then that he heard a shot and Joan crying out: 'Fetch help quickly, it's hurting.' As he left the summerhouse to get help, Croft heard a second shot, ran back and found she had shot herself a second time. 'I then took the pistol meaning to shoot myself but I could not do it.'

He added that when he told the duty officer: 'I have killed Joan', he had meant he felt responsible for her death, and not that he had killed her himself.

In his closing speech to the jury, Mr Edmunds suggested that after firing the first shot into her chest, Joan had fallen to the floor and may have dropped the gun, the impact of it hitting the floor accidentally firing the second shot which killed her.

The judge advised the jury that suicide was 'self-murder' and that if Joan Lewis had killed herself, she had committed murder. If Croft had aided her in any way, then he was as guilty of murder as if he had shot her himself.

It was a bizarre case riddled with a lot of conjecture and contradictions but the jury took only 25 minutes to reach a verdict – they found Croft guilty of murder and he was sentenced to hang.

Yet that was not the end of the matter. Croft's legal team lodged an appeal on the grounds that the judge has not properly directed the jury - that he had failed to advise them of the possibility that the fatal second shot could have been accidental. The defence also claimed that the survivor of a suicide pact could not be convicted of murder if they were not present when the other participant took their own life. Croft had testified he had left the summerhouse before the second shot.

The Appeal Court rejected the suggestion the jury had been mis-directed, and also the claim that as Croft wasn't present when the second shot was fired, he was not therefore aiding a suicide. The judges said that even if Croft wasn't in the summerhouse, he had left a loaded gun in the presence of Joan Lewis and that in itself meant he aided or abetted her as defined in law.

However, in a surprising twist, the appeal court appeared to show some sympathy for Croft – they commuted his death sentence to life imprisonment. Some years later he was released and appears to have disappeared back into society.

Recalling the case in his autobiography many years later, pathologist Dr Denis Hocking revealed a piece of evidence that was not presented at Croft's trial. Hocking said that the Webley gun used to kill Joan used 0.455 calibre bullets and two had been fired. However, a third bullet in the chamber had marks showing that two attempts were made to fire it, but the bullet in the chamber had jammed. The reason was that it was 0.450, the wrong size and meant for use in a Smith and Wesson revolver. Hocking said this may have been evidence that Croft had indeed tried to shoot himself – as he said he had – before going to get help for Joan. Hocking believed that the killing of Joan Lewis was probably 'a suicide pact gone wrong'.

That was far from the end of the story of the dramatic wartime shooting in the summerhouse at Housel Bay Hotel. Thirty-five years later, in 1978, friends of Dr Hocking, the pathologist who gave evidence at the trial, purchased Housel Bay Hotel. Even as the transaction was taking place, Mr and Mrs Stanley, the new owners, were informed that there had been numerous sightings of the ghost of a young woman in Women's Auxiliary Air Force uniform walking around the hotel gardens!

Mr Stanley was rather sceptical of these tales and he and his wife completed the purchase of the hotel in April. However, they were not prepared for what happened just a few months later.

On October 6, a guest at the hotel - a woman from Stockport in Cheshire who was on the second day of a four-day break – came in from the gardens crying and in a very distressed state. Mr and Mrs Stanley tried to calm her and when she recovered her composure, she told them that she had encountered a woman in the gardens who was weeping and had told her she was Joan Lewis and that she was waiting for her lover to join her as he has promised in their suicide pact.

Even more astonishing was that the lady from Stockport said she had arranged to meet the young woman again the following evening! The next night, Mr Stanley lead the woman by torchlight to a bench in the garden where the rendezvous was due to take place, and on her instructions left her alone and went back to the hotel. Some fifteen minutes later, the woman returned, again deeply upset and said she would write down details of the conversation that she said had taken place between her and girl.

Mr Stanley read the notes and found all the details of names, dates and times relating to the 1943 murder were correct. He said the woman told him she had never been to Cornwall before and had no prior knowledge of the murder which had taken place in the hotel grounds 35 years earlier.

The incident could perhaps have been dismissed as the ramblings of an over-emotional woman who had perhaps read something about the case, but the following year there was another extraordinary occurrence in the garden of the Housel Bay Hotel.

A couple from Sheffield were staying at the hotel and the husband was a commercial artist who designed decorative tiles and also sketched as a hobby. One afternoon he returned from the garden saying he had seen a young woman in an WAAF uniform in the garden and enquired if she was a guest at the hotel. Mr Stanley decided not to mention the Joan Lewis case, he merely said the woman was not a guest. But a couple of days later, the man again came in from the garden saying he had seen the same girl in uniform sitting on a bench. As she looked rather sad, he decided not to go over to speak to her.

Mr Stanley did not take him seriously. 'I told him I thought he was pulling my leg,' he said. However, to his surprise the man said the girl was definitely there because he had just sketched her, and opening the sketch pad he always carried with him, showed Mr Stanley a drawing of a young woman in a 1940 WAAF uniform sitting on the garden bench.

Since then, there have been no further 'ghostly' sightings recorded, but those that were reported form a sad postscript to a very tragic murder.

Leaving aside the bizarre ghostly aspect of the shooting of Joan Lewis, it is an extraordinary and puzzling case.

Only two people were in the summerhouse that night. Either William Croft couldn't face the reality of Joan going away and in a highly emotional state shot her, then panicked and concocted a cover story, or Joan was first to shoot herself but because the bullet failed to kill her, Croft shot her to complete the job. Then he tried to shoot himself, but the gun jammed.

The fact that the third bullet in the chamber of the revolver was the wrong size and had jammed was inexplicably never raised at the trial. If it had, it could have had some effect on the outcome, for it clearly showed Croft had tried to shoot himself – there were two hammer marks on the cartridge.

Dr Denis Hocking was a Harley Street consultant before becoming the Cornwall County Pathologist and in a long career examined an astonishing 35,000 dead bodies, many of them murder, accident or suicide victims. His long experience and his detailed account of the murder of Joan Lewis led him to conclude her death was the result of a 'suicide pact gone wrong'. I think he was right.

CONFESSION

When an elderly pub landlady in Portsmouth was found murdered and the bar takings stolen, the police were quick to act, making house to house inquiries and pulling in known local criminals for questioning. Their efforts initially produced no results and as the year was 1943 and the town was on alert for raids by German bombers targeting ports along England's south coast, the police had to scale down their inquiries into the murder of 63-year-old Rose Robinson, who had run the John Barleycorn pub in Commercial Road, Portsmouth for many years. It had been a particularly savage crime which had occurred on the night on November 28th, which was a Sunday,

Rose Robinson had run the pub for over 30 years, initially with her husband and then after he died eleven years earlier, had become the licensee herself. She was very popular but perhaps a little too trusting, for it was well known among the regulars that she kept the bar taking in her bedroom and banked them only at the end of each month. The John Barleycorn was a very busy pub and a month's taking would have totalled about £400 - equal to around £18,000 in today's money. On that Sunday evening, the pub closed at 10pm and having ensured all the doors and windows were locked, Mrs Robinson went upstairs, taking the money from the till with her.

Exactly what happened after that is not clear but when at around 9am the next morning the pub's cleaning lady arrived and had no response to her knocking the door, she asked a neighbour to climb the wall at the rear of the house. He found the back door open, went inside and let in the cleaner and together they began looking for Rose Robinson. They found her lying dead on the bedroom floor.

It was apparent the room had been ransacked. A blackout curtain had been torn down, drawers had been opened and contents strewn around, and two handbags and a purse lay on the bed, all empty. Rose has been strangled, and bruises and cuts indicated she had put up a fight. Pathologist Keith Simpson examined the scene and suggested that on her seeing or hearing an intruder, she had most probably tried to get to the window to shout for help but had been overpowered and the blackout curtain ripped down during a struggle.

He said marks on Rose's neck indicated she was strangled primarily by the pressure of a strong right hand and that her attacker was probably sitting astride her at the time, pinning her to the floor.

While police activity had been intense in the immediate aftermath of the murder, their inquiries had petered out given the wartime demand on police resources. However, just three weeks after the murder, the police got a lucky break, not in Portsmouth but in London. Two plain-clothed officers on duty in Waterloo Road, South East London, were specifically looking for people who might be handling stolen property. They noticed a rather scruffy man go into a cafe and trying to sell a pair of what appeared to be brand new shoes.

The man was Henry Loughans, aged 47 and of no fixed address. When challenged by the police, he at first claimed the shoes had belonged to his brother and as they didn't fit, he was trying to sell them. The officers didn't believe him and when told he was being arrested on suspicion of having stolen goods. Loughans didn't seemed to too concerned and told them: 'I'm wanted for things far more serious than this.'

On arriving at Kennington Road police station, Loughans became distressed, started to cry and then blurted out an astonishing story.

He said: ' I've been through hell in the past three weeks. I've been a bastard all my life and I'll finish as I lived. I was sorry from the moment I'd done it. I haven't slept since; it's preyed on my mind. She must have had a weak heart, the poor old girl.'

Still emotional and very upset, he then admitted carrying out a number of robberies in and around London but then added: 'I did the big job at Portsmouth where I got the money when I strangled the old woman at the beer-house.' He said he had given the stolen money to a woman accomplice who was waiting outside the pub and that the two of them had then driven back to London.

The Metropolitan police knew of the Portsmouth pub murder, it had generated widespread news coverage, so they immediately asked Loughans if he would make a formal statement, which he did.

In it, he said he was in Portsmouth the previous month and had been in a pub talking to customers and had learned that the landlady Rose Robinson always keep the pub taking in her bedroom above the pub. He said he couldn't recall the name of the pub but it was in Commercial Road and that the next night he broke in through a rear window and went upstairs where he saw a woman aged about 60. In his statement, he said: 'I grabbed her and told her to keep quiet. She screamed and I put my hands around her throat. She became quiet and I thought she had fainted. I left her on the floor, and I found a lot of money, mostly in five-pound notes.'

Loughans said he did not intend to kill Rose, only stop her screaming, and that he had arrived in Portsmouth in a car he had hired in London, and used the car to return there.

Some of the smaller details of his account differed from those known to the police, but Loughans had admitted his memory was a bit hazy and he was distraught while giving his statement. But in the key essentials of the Portsmouth crime, including the date, the location, layout of the pub and where the money was kept, he was accurate so the Met alerted the Portsmouth police, who promptly sent a detective inspector and a sergeant to London, and they arrived at Kennington Road police station at 2am.

Loughans told the officers that his written statement was correct, and he voluntarily gave a verbal account of what happened at the pub. This time, more composed than previously, he filled in more details and was more accurate about the sequence of events. He again said he did not intend to kill Rose Robinson when he held her by the throat, he just thought she had fainted or perhaps had a weak heart.

The officers knew they had their man and put Loughans in their car and set off back to Portsmouth. Loughans slept most of the way but as the car sped into the Portsmouth suburbs he woke up and when they were within 50 metres of the John Barleycorn pub, he said: 'This is somewhere near the place.'

At Fratton police station he made another statement which while sometimes slightly inaccurate was very close to what the police knew had happened at the pub. Loughans confirmed he found the money in handbags, mostly in five-pound notes. He said his accomplice was waiting nearby in the hire car and they drove off. He refused to name the accomplice other than saying she was 'a young lady' nor would he say what type of car was used. He also said that the money stolen was about £450 which tallied with the police estimate. He claimed he had given most of the money to the girl to keep for him, but had told her to 'go away' if he was ever arrested.

The police had a full admission from Loughans in two written

35

statements and his verbal account and he was charged with the murder of Rose Robinson and remanded in custody. He did not ask for legal aid and said he would like to be tried as soon as possible.

There was also some significant forensic evidence to link Loughans to the crime scene. On his shoes and trousers were fibres similar to those on three different rugs in Rose's bedroom. There was also a small feather found on the sleeve of his coat similar to those in an eiderdown on Rose's bed.

The prosecution case was all set for trial but on January 6th there was a surprise development. Loughans, who was being held on remand, asked for an urgent meeting with the prison governor and declared he was innocent of the murder charge, but had been afraid to say so as he had received some of the stolen money. He said when making his written confessions, the police had puts words into his mouth. A week later at an interim court appearance he repeated that he was not guilty. Given his multiple admissions and the forensic evidence, the prosecution was very confident their case was strong although they were somewhat bemused by his sudden change of plea. However, that bemusement was soon to turn into shock.

The first inkling came at the opening of the trial at Hampshire Assizes on March 14th 1944. As the barristers were getting ready and were about to make their entrance into the courtroom, Loughans' QC John Maude told prosecuting counsel Joshua Casswell: 'I am going to call completely independent witnesses who will provide Loughans with an alibi.'

Recalling that moment in his autobiography published 16 years later, Casswell admits he was stunned. 'Do you mean to say you are going to try to prove Loughans wasn't even in Portsmouth on the night of the murder?" he asked.

'That's right,' said Maude.

The trial opened and Loughans pleaded not guilty. Having outlined the background details and the sequence of events on the night of the murder, the prosecution called pathologist Dr Keith Simpson who said marks on Rose's throat indicated she had been strangled, primarily by the strong sustained grip of a right hand.

And although Loughans right hand had four fingers partially severed after an accident, Simpson told the court he was certain the deformed hand would still have had enough power to perform the strangulation, using the thumb and knuckle joints.

So far, the prosecution case was on track, but then a police officer detailing Loughans criminal background told the court that three years earlier in 1941, Loughans had confessed to a murder in Scotland but investigations established his confession to be totally false.

This was a tiny crack in the prosecution's case but it was a signal of far worse to come.

Loughans counsel John Maude rose to his feet and in effect shattered the prosecution case in just 60 words: 'On the night of the murder, my client was in Warren Street Underground Station in London. You are going to see witnesses who were in that station,' he said. 'There are three women, who when interviewed, were able to remember this man quite distinctly. Remembering Loughans would not be difficult. He has a distinctive face and a hand that nobody would forget.'

The Warren Street station was used at night as an air-raid shelter with many people crammed into it. All three women remembered Loughans because of his hand. One said Loughans slept two bunks away from her and that in the night she had got up and covered him with a raincoat. Another woman said she had loaned him a pillow and a third clearly recalled talking to him about a visit to Huddersfield, and she had noticed his missing fingers. As if that wasn't enough of a blow for the prosecution, a London Transport track-layer told the court he remembered Loughans talking to the women and particularly noticed his deformed hand. When he asked how he was so sure it was the Sunday night of the murder he said Sunday was the only day they laid tracks or made repairs. And another railway worker produced a 'Record Of Works' book which confirmed that track laying took place only on November 28-29, which was the Sunday night Rose Robinson was murdered.

Prosecuting counsel Joshua Casswell later recalled: 'I was not at all sanguine about the outcome. After all, no man can be in two places at once.'

When cross-examined, Loughans - who had an extensive criminal record and had been to prison several times - told the court he had confessed to the murder in Scotland to give police 'a little bit of trouble' because he felt they had been harassing him, and that he confessed to the murder of Rose Robinson as 'a hoax and a grand joke'.

He explained his knowledge of the Robinson murder came from newspaper reports and also from the police themselves while questioning him. He said the police often gave him details of the case and the answers to their questions 'at the same time'.

The prosecution team tried to undermine this claim by saying the Met police who first questioned Loughans would not have full knowledge of the Portsmouth case. However, later in the defence submission, John Maude was quick to point out that while there were inaccuracies in the statement Loughans gave to the Met, his later statement to Portsmouth police gave more precise information which he could have obtained only from his conversations with the Portsmouth police officers.

The jury members were so confused with all they had heard as this remarkable case had unfolded, they were unable to reach a verdict and so a re-trial began just two weeks later on April 4th at the Old Bailey before a new judge and jury, but with the same prosecution and defence lawyers.

The evidence was largely a repeat of the first trial, but defence counsel John Maude produced a new witness, the famous and authoritative pathologist Sir Bernard Spilsbury who immediately rejected the findings of the prosecution pathologist Keith Simpson who had insisted that Loughans crippled hand could still have the strength to strangle Rose Robinson.

Simpson - who surprisingly also wrote crime fiction under the pseudonym Guy Bailey - was forced to concede he had not actually examined Loughans hand, he had merely seen a plaster cast of it. And as Spilsbury very convincingly pointed out to the jury, Simpson could not know from just a plaster cast of the hand that in the machinery accident that had severed Loughans fingers, much of the muscle tissue in his arm was also torn away, resulting in him having almost no power in his right hand. Spilsbury said he doubted if Loughans hand was strong enough 'to cause even a scratch.'

That, along with Loughans cast-iron alibi and the forensic evidence found at the murder scene shown to be only similar rather than identical, the prosecution case collapsed. The jury took less than an hour to find Harold Loughans not guilty.

However, it turned out to be a rather hollow victory for the man who so disliked the police he had tried to show them to be incompetent and get even with them by making false confessions. Just a few weeks later, Harold Loughans was behind bars having been convicted of an unrelated burglary.

Whoever did murder Rose Robinson and stole the pub takings on that fateful November night was never caught. At least not officially.

Twenty years later in 1963, Harold Loughans sued The People newspaper for libel after it published part of the memoirs of Joshua Casswell who was the prosecuting counsel in the Rose Robinson murder case. Loughans claimed that comments by Casswell in his book implied he did murder the pub landlady despite the fact a jury had acquitted him. But the libel jury rejected Loughans claim.

Even that was not the end of this extraordinary matter for just a few months later, Harold Loughans, now aware he had terminal cancer and also knowing he could not be tried for the same offence twice, walked into the office of The People newspaper and made a full confession, admitting that he had murdered Rose Robinson.

It is hard to determine whether this belated confession was true or was perhaps made for publicity reasons or - much more likely - for a payment from the newspaper. In the late 1960s, I worked as a freelance contributor to The People, and while I don't recall this specific case, I know it was then common practice for the newspaper to make very substantial payments for such exclusive stories.

Given the strength of witness evidence at Loughans original trial that he was elsewhere at the time of the murder, in my view his final confession has to be treated with scepticism.

Whatever the truth of the matter, just two years later in 1965, Harold Loughans died at the age of 69. A persistent liar and hardened criminal, he had spent 23 years of his life in prison - though none of them related to the murder of Rose Robinson.

THE RELUCTANT JUDGE

Joseph Williams, a man who was penniless and about to be evicted from his lodging, went to visit an old friend who was very wealthy. Just a few hours later, the old friend was found battered to death in his own home, his safe robbed of cash and jewellery. So it was no surprise that Joseph Williams was top of the list of suspects.

That suspicion was confirmed when forensic tests showed that Williams' thumb-print was on a beer glass in the victim's home, banknotes Williams had in his possession were traced to the victim's bank, and cigarette stubs found at the murder scene contained saliva from someone with the same rare blood group as Williams. They also found that Williams had no alibi for the time the murder was committed.

Despite this weight of evidence, when police arrested Williams and charged him with murder, he was remarkably cheerful. 'The whole thing is ridiculous,' he said, smiling as he posed in handcuffs for Press photographers. 'Everyone will be astounded.'

It may be that people who knew him were astounded, but any astonishment at that time would seem microscopic compared with the astounding event that was to take place a few weeks later when he went on trial for murder.

This headline-grabbing case had begun in Poole, Dorset on May 20th 1939. Relatives of local businessman Walter Dinnivan returned to his apartment to find him lying in a pool of blood on the floor, his head severely battered. He was rushed by ambulance to hospital where he died soon after arrival, never regaining consciousness.

Dinnivan was 64 years old, a former chairman of the local Conservative Party, and who owned several residential properties and a garage. He lived in the wealthy Branksome area of Poole in an apartment with his 18-year-old grand-daughter, who acted as his housekeeper. She and Dinnivan's grandson had been out for the evening and discovered his body when they returned about 11 pm.

It had been a vicious attack. There were ten circular indentations in his skull suggesting blows from a hammer, and his nose and two ribs were also broken. There were also signs of attempted strangulation.

The motive was evident – Dinnivan's wallet was missing, as were two gold rings and a silver watch he was wearing. And his safe had been opened with his own key and a quantity of cash was missing, as were several items of jewellery which had belonged to his late wife.

Detectives began a detailed search of the apartment and on a table, they found two glasses and a beer bottle. It was known Dinnivan never drank beer and when the glasses were finger-printed, one of them bore a thumb-print which was not from Dinnivan. There were also four cork-tipped cigarettes found in the room, and Dinnivan never smoked that type of cigarette. Police also found a blood-stained paper bag and an imitation tortoise-shell hair-curler of unusual design. This latter item turned out to be a red herring as while it was discovered Dinnivan sometimes had prostitutes visit his apartment, enquiries eventually discounted the hair-curler as a significant clue.

Police learned from neighbours and from Dinnivan's grand-daughter that a man called Joseph Williams was a long-standing friend of Dinnivan, had sometimes borrowed money from him and had visited the apartment a few days earlier. Williams, who was 70, was a former army officer who had become near-destitute after a series of unwise business ventures and was now reduced to living in a bedsit with just a camp bed, a chair and a table.

When police interviewed Williams, he readily admitted he had been to Dinnivan's flat just two or three days before the murder, and told police he had borrowed £5 (about £330 in today's money) from Dinnivan, who had also shown him his late wife's jewellery. But he denied having been in the flat on the night of the murder.

He said on that evening, he had been in his bedsit until 8.30 pm after which he walked into Bournemouth -a distance of five miles) – and strolled around for a while along the seafront and pier and then caught a bus back to Poole, arriving at his bedsit at 11.30 pm to bed. He then went to bed. However, he could not produce any witnesses to confirm his movements and he was arrested and charged with murder.

At Poole magistrates court, Williams pleaded not guilty and his lawyer put forward alternative explanations to counter the prosecution evidence but the court felt the matter must go to trial.

The trial opened at Dorchester Assizes on October 11th and the judge was Mr Justice Croom-Johnson, only recently appointed to the judiciary but notable as prosecuting counsel in the famous Rattenbury murder trial four years earlier.

Joshua Casswell – who had also featured in the famous Rattenbury trial as defence counsel - now appeared as prosecutor and was confident of getting a conviction as he felt the evidence against Williams was overwhelming.

Casswell presented a strong case, telling the jury that as Williams was destitute, he had visited his wealthy friend Walter Dinnivan with the clear intention of robbing him. While the men enjoyed a drink, Williams produced a hammer from a paper bag and attacked his friend causing several head wounds, and then inflicted other injuries to ensure he was dead and could not identify his attacker.

Cross-examined by Casswell, Williams was confident and convincing, denying he was at the flat on the night of the murder. He said his thumb-print on the beer glass was because the glass hadn't been washed since his visit a couple of days earlier. Challenged about saliva on the cigarette stubs being from someone with his rare blood group, he countered by saying that would still leave many other people who could be suspects. As for the blood-stained paper bag – which police had found had a distinct manufacturing fault and was identical to several found in Williams bedsit, he claimed this was just coincidence – there would have been thousands of such bags made. And of banknotes found on him which had serial numbers traced to Dinnivan's bank, Williams pointed out that was not significant as Dinnivan had loaned him cash previously.

After Casswell's forceful cross-examination of Williams, there was a surprise development. The judge, Mr Justice Croom-Johnson, who had been seen shaking his head and tutting from time to time while Williams was in the witness box, suddenly invited the jury to dismiss the case!

The judge clearly favoured Williams' account of events and seemed remarkably sympathetic towards him. 'You have heard this man and seem him in the box,' he told the jury. 'Recollect that the prosecution has to establish a case for your satisfaction without any reasonable doubt.'

He said none of the evidence against Williams was conclusive and that if the jury agreed with that, they could end the case there and then. The shocked jury asked for time to consider the matter but they returned in just five minutes to say they wished the case to continue.

Yet after all the evidence had been heard and the prosecution and defence counsel had made their closing statements, Mr Justice Croom-Johnson again showed he favoured the version of events given by Joseph Williams. In his summing up, he reminded the jury that the murder weapon had never been found, nor had the missing jewellery. He pointed out that there was no evidence that Williams smoked cork-tipped cigarettes and that even though Williams blood group was rare, there were still 15,000 other people in the area with that same blood group.

And just in case the jury hadn't got his message, Mr Justice Croom-Johnson pointedly told them it was better for dozens of guilty people to escape justice that for one innocent person to be convicted!
The bewildered jury went out to discuss the matter and returned 70 minutes later to declare they found Joseph Williams not guilty.

Almost two decades later, soon after Judge Croom-Johnson died in the late 1950s, and there was no risk of being sued for libel, prosecuting counsel Joshua Casswell published his memoirs in which he candidly stated that he felt the judge was prejudiced in favour of Williams. 'I have never known a judge exhibit so strong a pro-defence inclination,' he said, adding that he believed the case was the first murder trial over which Croom-Johnson had presided and that he seemed 'very reluctant' to put on the black cap and pass the death sentence, perhaps because of the age of the defendant. Williams was 70 years old at the time.

Whatever the reason, it was a sensational end to a sensational trial and the popular Sunday newspaper the News Of The World had signed-up Williams for an exclusive interview and took him away to a local hotel.

Yet the biggest sensation was still to come.

During his interview at the hotel with Norman Rae, the News Of The World reporter, Williams was forthright and quite arrogant, telling Rae that he had always been certain he would be found not guilty and had actually enjoyed trying to outwit the police. 'It was so preposterous when the detectives seemed to suspect me that I thought I would have a little joke,' he said. 'It was my fault entirely that in some ways I tried to mislead them. But can you blame me? I knew from the very beginning I was completely innocent.'

He said he and Dinnivan had been friends since childhood. 'I was proud to call him my friend. We never had a cross word at any time,' he said.

Questioned further by Rae, Williams admitted he had 'been a bit of a fool' in business and was very short of money. He said: 'What was more natural than for me think of my old friend, who so far as I knew was still prosperous, hoping that he would offer to help. I am certain that if someone had not killed him, he would have come to my aid.'

Norman Rae filed his story and then went to bed. But in the early hours of the morning, he heard loud knocking on his bedroom door and when he opened it, there stood Joseph Williams, very distressed and sobbing.

'I've got to tell somebody,' said Williams. 'The jury was wrong. It was me. I killed Walter Dinnivan. Now I've told you, I feel better, I'll be able to sleep now.'

Norman Rae was stunned, but uncertain what to do next. He knew there was no point in telling the police – the law at that time was clear than no one could be tried again for a crime for which they had already been acquitted, even if they had since confessed. And the only evidence of the confession was from Rae himself – and in the cold light of day, Williams would probably deny it.

At breakfast, Williams was his usual cheerful self, joking about being found not guilty. He didn't mention his visit to Norman Rae's room in the early hours, and Rae knew there was nothing he could do but stay silent.

Rae kept his secret for twelve years until 1951 when he heard that Williams had died at his home in Nottingham. Then Rae felt he had to put the record straight. He added another sensational aspect to an already sensational murder case by publishing the confession, but knowing it had no legal validity and that in law at least, Joseph Williams would still be regarded as an innocent man.

People confessing to crimes they did not commit is not uncommon. Sometimes it is done merely to seek attention or to waste police time to get even for some past encounter with them. And sometimes confessions are made to protect the real culprit, perhaps a friend or a family member.

The motive for Joseph Williams' confession is difficult to categorise. He was a cunning man who would probably have been clever enough, had he murdered his friend, to have left no clues at all. He would not have been careless enough to leave his thumb print on a glass or leave a blood-stained paper bag at the scene. However, he was also arrogant and very plausible and may have just felt he could talk his way out of any difficult situation, which in effect is what he did in court. He was able to convince a judge and jury that despite circumstantial evidence, he was innocent of the murder.

His late-night confession to Norman Rae seems to have been the result of too much to drink and attention-seeking bravado - but it could well have been the truth.

Whoever murdered Walter Dinnivan must have known him. They clearly knew he had money and jewellery in his flat and they knew him well enough to be let in and even offered a drink. Williams ticks all those boxes and there were no other suspects but in law, the burden of proof has to be 'beyond reasonable doubt' and this this case it was not.

THE ACID TEST

When someone is convinced they have discovered a method of committing the perfect murder and are bold enough to try it out with an actual killing, you may think that when they succeed in proving their theory, they might decide that once is enough.

But John Haigh was not just someone. He was clever, extremely charming and confident but also totally emotionless. He showed a depth of cold-hearted indifference many would describe as pure evil, and he went on to become a multiple murderer.

Haigh was raised in Yorkshire by parents who belonged to the strict religious sect the Plymouth Brethren and he received a good education, studying science and divinity and was an excellent student who also sang in the school choir. But in 1931 when Haigh was 22 years old, the amiable young man with a steady job at an insurance company suddenly turned to crime.

The catalyst was an incident in the office where he worked – a cash box was missing and Haigh was suspected though no evidence was found. Even so, Haigh was promptly dismissed and he took the opportunity to review his career options. He decided his personable nature and friendly charm could be combined with two other strong talents would enable him to embark on a new career.

One of his talents was that he found it easy to be a convincing liar. The other was even more useful – he had an uncanny natural ability to copy handwriting with perfect precision, so Haigh decided to become a professional fraudster. To him it was a logical and natural decision. He later explained that he turned to fraud because it was easier working long hours in an office: 'I didn't ask myself whether it was right or wrong. That seemed to me to be irrelevant.'

He began with a series of small insurance frauds and as he became more confident, he became more ambitious and was soon in a financial position which enabled him to have smart clothing and an eye-catching red sports car. Dark-haired, good looking and well-spoken, he had several attractive girlfriends and one of them was a 21-year-old model called Betty Hamer, who he married in secret at a registry office in Bridlington in the summer of 1934.

It was a very short relationship. Just four months later, Betty's dreams of an idyllic marriage were shattered when police arrested Haigh on fraud charges and he was sent for trial at Leeds Assizes. Haigh had devised a scheme to obtain a supply of hire-purchase forms from a finance company and then used his forgery skills to apply for multiple loans to buy cars that were never purchased. The scheme was so successful that Haigh engaged a couple of friends to help him, but when the fraud was uncovered, police identified Haigh as the ring leader and when he was convicted, he was given a fifteen-month prison sentence.

When he was released from Wakefield prison, Haigh, now 27 years old, left Yorkshire for London and got a job as a secretary and chauffeur to a wealthy businessman but after a year, left to set up a new fraudulent scheme he had been devising. He created three fictitious legal firms, had stationary printed and sent out more than 400 letters across the UK saying the legal firms were acting for clients who needed to dispose of high-value shares at a discounted price. Eager buyers sent in their cheques and within a week, Haigh had raised £1,050 – about £70,000 in today's money.

He planned to disappear with the money, assuming that his use of fake names and addresses would cover his trail. But he was wrong, the police caught up with him and this time, the court handed down a four-year sentence to be served in Dartmoor Prison.

Released on licence after three years, Haigh found himself in wartime Britain. It was 1940 and Haigh was 31. He was called up join the forces but he kept moving address so the call-up papers never reached him. Finding it tough to make a living, he resorted to petty theft from his landlady, who reported him to the police. As he was still on licence, Haigh was sent to Lincoln prison serve another 21 months.

While there, he used the prison library to study legal, technical and scientific subjects and when he was released in 1943, decided to use his new-found knowledge to create a potentially lucrative new career – murder.

Haigh had obtained a job in the prison metalwork shop where sulphuric acid was used to treat various metals and Haigh was able to steal small amounts of acid which he used to immerse mice which were supplied to him by trustee prisoners who worked in nearby fields. Haigh had used tobacco to bribe them to get mice for his experiments. What Haigh discovered was that a mouse put in a jar of acid would dissolve completely - not even the bones remained - and he decided that a human body could be dissolved without trace by the same process.

Soon after being released from prison, Haigh found a job as a book-keeper and salesman at a small engineering firm in Crawley, Sussex. After a few months there, he left for London where he rented accommodation in Kensington and quickly set up a fake company called Union Group Engineering, described as a specialist consultancy with him as its liaison officer. The headed paper stated the company had branches in Croydon and more significantly in Crawley, where Haigh had been working a few months earlier.

Even more significantly, Haigh also took a lease on a basement near his lodgings and began to secretly store a substantial number of large glass containers filled with sulphuric acid. They were easy to obtain as he had - on headed notepaper at least - an engineering firm. His next step was to find a suitable victim.

London was in a wartime blackout so it was easy to move around virtually unnoticed while looking for a victim yet it was by chance while drinking in The Goat pub in Kensington High Street that Haigh met an ideal candidate for murder, an old friend he had worked with some years earlier.

The man was William McSwan who had sold the lucrative family business operating amusement arcades and had invested the money in five houses which he and his parents rented out. Haigh saw an opportunity and quickly cultivated the friendship, learning that McSwan was trying to dodge being called up for army service. When McSwan happened to mention he was looking for storage for a quantity of redundant pinball machines, Haigh was gifted an opportunity. He said he had the ideal storage location - his nearby basement premises. He took McSwan and once inside the building he clubbed him to death with a lead pipe. While searching the body, he found the keys to McSwan's flat and aware that McSwan and his parents also owned five other properties, devised a plan to get his hands on them all. But first, he had to dispose of McSwan's body.

Haigh had a large oil drum which had been used as a water butt and he forced the body into it and then filled the drum with several gallons of sulphuric acid, sealing it with a lid. Two days later when he returned to the basement and opened the drum, he found his calculations were correct - the body had completed dissolved. He then emptied the slurry from the drum into the drainage system, thus removing all traces of the gruesome murder.

Haigh was always well-dressed, his dark hair neatly parted and swept back and he had a small and at that time fashionable moustache. This smart presentable image helped him dupe people, for he exuded great confidence and charm. And the next part of Haigh's plan certainly required his skills as a convincing fraudster. He went to see William McSwan's elderly parents in Pimlico, knowing that they were aware that their son was trying to avoid being called up by the army. Introducing himself as a friend of William, Haigh told the old couple William had gone to Scotland for a while to avoid his call-up papers. Haigh was so convincing he was even able to persuade the old couple to allow him to take over the collecting of rents from their properties, a role previously carried out by their son.

In the weeks that followed, Haigh underpinned his lie by making several trips to Glasgow, each time sending McSwan's parents' postcards and letters apparently from their son, whose handwriting he could imitate with ease. They never suspected anything and considered Haigh to be a perfect gentleman and valued friend of their son.

Feeling the couple now trusted him completely, Haigh felt it was time to order two new 40-gallon oil-drums.

Once the drums were installed in the basement, Haigh told Donald McSwan that his son, who was still dodging military call-up, was returning to London and that the basement would be a good place for a secret meeting with him. McSwan agreed and went with Haigh. As soon as they were in the basement, Haigh killed McSwan and immediately went back to Pimlico to lure Mrs McSwan with the same story. Back in the basement, she too was immediately killed and the two bodies were placed in drums of sulphuric acid and days later, completely dissolved, were flushed down into the sewers.

Haigh, smartly-attired and well-spoken, then convinced the McSwan's neighbours that the couple had gone to live in America and that he had been granted power of attorney to settle their affairs and dispose of their properties.

In a matter of weeks, Haigh, using fake letters of authority and perfectly-forged signatures was able to sell the McSwan's five houses and empty their bank accounts, netting him £6,000 – the equivalent of around £430,000 in today's money.

For the two years after the second world war ended, Haigh indulged in a lavish lifestyle, residing in a Kensington hotel, wearing tailor-made suits, driving an expensive Lagonda Convertible, and going to the theatre and the opera. He also tried to establish several new engineering businesses but they all failed and towards the end of 1947, Haigh was broke.

Perhaps not surprisingly, he decided the simple solution for his financial problems was to find another wealthy couple to murder and again dispose of the bodies in acid. And he knew just such a couple, Dr Archie Henderson and his wife Rose. Haigh had met them while looking at house they were selling, and again his charming personality was irresistible. While he didn't intend to buy the house, just use the viewing as an excuse to identify potential victims, he made such an impression on them they started inviting him to house parties and he soon became a good friend of the couple.

When in early1948 Archie and Rose decided to take a short winter break at the Metropole Hotel in Brighton, Haigh saw his chance, He had a small workshop in Crawley in Sussex - a legacy of his previous failed business partnership – and it was just 22 miles from Brighton.

Again, Haigh's powers of persuasion came into play. He told Archie Henderson that he had a small business making powder-compacts and there was a potentially lucrative investment opportunity available.

He added that as the premises were only a 30-minute drive away, Archie could take a look while Rose remained at the hotel. Archie agreed. Soon after arrival at the Crawley workshop Haigh shot Henderson through the head, using a gun he had previously stolen from Archie's home while the couple were away. The workshop was in an enclosed yard used for storage and people in nearby houses were used to banging and clattering so a single shot did not attract attention. Packing Archie into a drum and filling it with acid, he returned to the Metropole Hotel in Brighton and told Archie's wife Rose that her husband had been taken ill and had been left in the care of a friend. Haigh then offered to drive Rose to see her husband and Rose readily agreed. Once at the workshop, Haigh shot Rose and put her into a drum of acid alongside the drum containing the fast-disappearing remains of her husband.

Haigh then rang the Metropole Hotel. Faking a woman's voice to impersonate Rose Henderson, he said an urgent matter had cropped up and she and her husband would not be returning to the hotel.

Haigh knew the couple had taken their Red Setter dog with them to Brighton so still posing as Rose, he asked the hotel to take care of the dog until the next day when someone would collect it.

Bizarrely, though Haigh had not shown the slightest compunction about killing humans, when he collected the dog, he didn't kill it. He kept it as his own pet.

Over the next few weeks, Haigh systematically acquired not only the Henderson's money but also a block of flats and a shop they owned. Despite family members being suspicious of Haigh, he was able to succeed in convincing them that Archie and Rose had left to make a new start in South America, and supported his story with letters he had written in Rose's hand-writing, along with various forged documents showing the couple had signed over their properties to him, along with all their personal effects. It was a masterly exercise in forgery and sheer bravado and the documents were even verified as genuine by a lawyer.

Once in possession of the properties, Haigh sold them all, bringing him around £500,000 in today's money. Yet just six months later, he had squandered the lot on high-living, failed business ventures and reckless gambling. He needed another wealthy victim.

He quickly found one at the hotel where he was resident - the Onslow Court Hotel in Kensington. Among other residents was 69-year-old Olive Durand-Deacon, a wealthy woman fond of showing off her expensive fur coat and gold and diamond jewellery. Haigh had chatted to her many times as their tables were adjoining in the hotel dining room, and so it was easy to talk her into the idea of her investing money in a new business he said he was setting up.

Haigh spent a couple of days re-equipping his Crawley workshop with a new 45-gallon oil drum and gallons of sulphuric acid and when everything was ready, he returned to the hotel and arranged to take Olive to his so-called business premises. Keen not to be seen leaving the hotel with Olive, he had arranged to meet her by the Army and Navy Store in Victoria and he picked her up there in his Alvis convertible and drove to his workshop in Leopold Road, Crawley.

Within minutes of Olive entering the building, Haigh shot her in the head, methodically gathered up her cash, jewellery,

diamond watch and fur coat, and then put her body in the drum. Before adding the acid, Haigh calmly popped out for poached eggs and toast at a nearby cafe. Suitably replenished, he returned to the workshop to fill the drum with acid. Later, having stopped to have dinner, he returned to his hotel in Kensington.

His next step would be to try to get his hands on Olive Durand-Deacon's fortune – estimated in today's money at around £2.4 million and mainly tied up in shares and other investments. But that would take time and desperate for cash, he began by selling her jewellery, netting him about £4,000 in today's money. And then something happened he had not anticipated.

With his previous murders Haigh had been able to allay the concerns of friends and relatives of the victims, so none of them had been reported missing to the police. But Olive Durand-Deacon had a close friend who was also resident at the Onslow Court Hotel, Mrs Constance Lane. And when Olive didn't return after two days, Mrs Lane announced to fellow guests that she intended to report the matter to the police. When Haigh heard this, while he was not much concerned about being found out given the success of his previous murders, he decided he ought to play up his role as a concerned friend and brazenly offered to drive Mrs Lane to Chelsea police station.

But Haigh's extraordinary luck was running out. A woman police sergeant, Maude Lambourne, who was noting the missing person details, seemed to see through Haigh's veneer of affability and charm and thought him worth checking out. Interviewing the hotel manager later, she learned Haigh was often late paying his bills and using that as a starting point she ran Haigh's name through the police files and discovered he had several convictions for fraud in the 1930s and early 1940s.

She alerted senior detectives who twice interviewed Haigh, who remained calm and helpful and boldly revealed his appointment with Olive the day she disappeared, saying he was due to take her to see one of his friends at an engineering firm in West Street, Crawley so they could discuss a business venture. He said he had arranged to pick her up at the Army and Navy Stores in Victoria at 2.30 pm but she never showed up.

Chelsea police asked the Sussex police in Horsham to check out the engineering firm Haigh had mentioned, which was still run by Haigh's former business associate Edward Jones, who had allowed Haigh to use the workshop in Leopold Street, a mile away from his own premises. Police officers interviewed Jones who confirmed he knew that Haigh was due to bring a potential client on the Friday, but the client hadn't shown up. There was no mention of Haigh's premises in Leopold Street and the police went away.

However, four days later a police sergeant at Horsham, Patrick Heslin, decided to make more enquires in Crawley and re-visited Edward Jones. During a casual conversation, Jones happened to mention that his firm had been started four years earlier at premises in Leopold Road, had then expanded and moved to its present site, and that the old premises were sometimes used for storage and development experiments by John Haigh.

Sergeant Heslin immediately realised the importance of this chance revelation and went straight to the Leopold Road workshop, forced the lock and went inside.

There he found large glass carboys of sulphuric acid, a pump, gas-mask, rubber boots and a rubber apron. At a glance, this in itself was not suspicious as all the items could have been legitimately used for metal treatments. But Haigh had become uncharacteristically careless. The detective sergeant also found a briefcase belonging to Haigh and in it were passports, driving licences and other documents in the names of McSwan and Henderson. Much more significantly, Heslin found a receipt from a local dry-cleaners for a women's fur coat. And in the bottom of the briefcase was a .38 revolver.

Hours later, Haigh was arrested and interviewed. While initially he tried to bluff it out, he seemed to realise further denial was futile. He confessed to murdering William McSwan and his parents, and Archie and Rose Henderson, and Olive Durand-Deacon. And while stunned police were recording the confession, Haigh coolly revealed there were three other victims too. And then he claimed that he had drunk the blood of the victims.

However, police were getting the measure of Haigh and felt these last confessions were false, just an attempt by him to signify mental illness that might get him a term the Broadmoor psychiatric hospital rather than an appointment with the hangman.

54

The arrest was national news and crowds lined the narrow street outside Horsham Magistrates Court when Haigh appeared and was charged with murder. The court building was a place I knew well, having worked as a journalist in the town in the early 1970s. The courtroom was just a few steps from my office.

Although he had confessed, John Haigh was convinced that the case against him might be hampered by there being a lack of evidence as all five bodies had dissolved. But he was wrong.

While at the basement in Kensington, Haigh had been able to pour the sludgy residue from the drums into the sewers, but there was no suitable drain at the Leopold Road workshop and being by then rather over-confident of his method, he had poured the residue over waste ground a few metres away from the building. While much of the residue had soaked away, forensic pathologist Keith Simpson and his team made a thorough search of the waste ground and initially found what they thought was a gall-stone. Inspired by the find, Simpson had 475 pounds of soil removed from the site for laboratory examination and the findings were dramatic.

He and his team found many lumps of body fat, bone fragments and even some false teeth still in good enough condition to later be identified by a dentist as belonging to Mrs Durand-Deacon.

The trial of John Haigh began at Lewes Assizes in July 1949 and took just two days. The defence counsel David Maxwell Fyfe did not cross examine witnesses and Haigh himself was not asked to give evidence. The reason for this was that the defence set out to prove that Haigh was insane and to support their case, they called an eminent Harley Street psychiatrist who said he believed Haigh was suffering from a rare form of paranoia and was not responsible for his actions. But his testimony was seriously undermined by intense cross-examination and the jury took only 17 minutes to find Haigh guilty of six murders, and he was sentenced to be hanged.

While held in prison awaiting execution, Haigh seemed to have accepted his fate and was reported to be quite relaxed. He even agreed to a request from Madame Tussaud's to take an impression of his face for use in creating a wax figure of him for display in their Chamber Of Horrors exhibition.

Rather flattered by the request and perhaps showing a touch of vanity,

Haigh also gave the museum one of his suits so his effigy would be as smartly dressed as he was. He stipulated that the suit should always be kept well-pressed, his shirt cuffs should always be showing, and his hair correctly parted.

John Haigh was hanged just a few days after his 40th birthday. Minutes before they were to put the noose around his neck he was asked if he wanted a brandy.

He nodded and said: 'Better make it a large one, old boy.'

DEATH ON WHEELS

It was a warm sunny July day when invalid Archibald Brown was taken out in his wheelchair by his nurse so he could enjoy some fresh air and country scenery but during their outing along a quiet residential lane just a mile from his home, the most extraordinary event took place. Mr Brown exploded.

A sudden blast blew him high into the air, severing his body at the waist. His lower body was blown to pieces and one leg was hurled 50 feet into a nearby garden and his other leg landed 15 feet up in the branches of tree.

The explosion also badly injured his nurse who was blown backwards several feet and the force of the blast also shattered windows in a nearby house.

The nurse, Elsie Mitchell, lay in the road with severe leg injuries and residents rushed to attend to her, and called an ambulance. Fortunately, the blast had been directed upwards so she had escaped its full force and survived.

The incident took place in Rayleigh in Essex, some six miles from Southend-on-Sea, and local police began an immediate investigation into the cause of the explosion and initially thought the blast was probably caused by a stray bomb as it was 1943 and German bombing raids were not uncommon along the Essex coast.

But that was quickly ruled out because forensic evidence at the scene revealed something far more sinister and led them to a discovery so shocking and so bizarre, they could scarcely believe it.

Police and explosive experts examined the road surface and the twisted remains of the wheelchair and quickly discovered that the explosion had not been caused by a stray bomb from an aircraft, nor had it been caused by the wheelchair striking an object that lay in the road.   What they did establish was that the blast which killed Archibald Brown was caused by some sort of explosive device that had been fitted under the cushion of his wheelchair. Brown's death was not a freak accident, it was a carefully-plotted murder.

An investigation began and both Archibald's wife Dorothy and their eldest son Eric, aged 19, were interviewed and said they were on good terms with Archibald, who had been in a wheelchair for several years because of a spinal injury. Mrs Brown said her husband could be very difficult when in pain, but at other times could be pleasant. The couple's other son, 16-year-old Colin, was away at boarding school at the time of the incident.

Police also interviewed Nurse Mitchell who was recovering well though would be left with some permanent disability to a leg and an arm. She said that there was no warning of the explosive, but significantly, said it occurred just as Mr Brown had moved his position on the seat.

This was further confirmation of an explosive device being fitted to the wheel chair, for not only had the upward direction of the blast been established by the wreckage of the wheelchair, but forensic examination of the road surface had located splinters of metal of a different type to that used on the wheelchair.

The hunt was now on for someone who either had a grudge against Archibald Brown, or who perhaps stood to benefit from his death. Brown was a wealthy man who owned a profitable grain mill in Rayleigh and he and his family lived in a large house on the outskirts of the town. They appeared to have a contented family life and no enemies.

Meantime, efforts were made by the police to identify the device used in the murder and it was eventually established that it was a Hawkins 75 anti-tank mine which by its nature, directed its blast vertically. However, such a device normally required pressure of 200-300 pounds in order to detonate, far more than the weight of Mr Brown. However, police found that anyone with specific technical knowledge would be able to adjust the detonation pressure to a much lower level. The police set out to discover who had access to an anti-tank mine, and also knew how to re-set it. And a potential suspect was quickly identified – Archibald Brown's eldest son Eric.

Although Eric was at that time working at his father's mill, he was actually on extended leave from the army where he had been given training on the assembly and ignition of mines - including the Hawkins 75 anti-tank model.

Eric was arrested and taken to Rayleigh Police Station where he was cautioned and interviewed. What he told police was an extraordinary story which had its roots in an incident that occurred 23 years earlier, before he was even born.

In 1920, Eric's father had been badly injured in a motorcycle crash which resulted in significant spinal damage. After a long period of recuperation, he was able to return to work at the family mill and in 1922 married his wife Dorothy and the couple had two children, Eric and Colin. But as the years passed, Archibald's spinal injury worsened and became increasing painful, and gradual paralysis also greatly restricted his mobility and confined him to a wheelchair. All this made him ill-tempered and very difficult to please. Even so, Mrs Brown did all she could for him and also engaged private nurses to help look after him.

Yet it was still evident to son Eric that his father's constant demands on his mother were often vindictive and cruel and becoming unbearable, though she bore them stoically and without complaint. But unknown to her, Eric had decided enough was enough.

He was able to smuggle out a Hawkins 75 mine from his army base by hiding it in a briefcase, and once he was back at home, in the privacy of the family air-raid shelter where the wheelchair was stored, he adjusted the pressure sensor to react to a lighter weight. He then attached the mine to the framework of the wheelchair directly under the seat cushion.

While it was possible the mine could have blown up when Mr Brown first sat in the chair, it actually went off during his outing, apparently triggered by him shifting position.

In the weeks after the murder, Mrs Brown had begun to suspect her son, having seen him come out of the air-raid shelter on the morning her husband had been killed. Asking Eric why he had been in the air-raid shelter, he said he had just been looking for a knife, and as he showed no sign of concern or upset at the question, she readily accepted his explanation.

Soon after, Eric was arrested and Mrs Brown realised she had been wrong about him and gave police candid details of the terrible life she and her son had to endure from her husband. She said her husband had always favoured their younger son Colin and so had constantly persecuted Eric when he was younger, often hitting him, locking him in a cupboard or a shed, made him write lines, prevented him for

59

going out to play and sometimes made him run up and down the hallway until he was exhausted.

Archibald Brown was also cruel to his wife, forbidding her to see her own mother, overturning food and drinks that she gave him, and had once grabbed her and tried to strangle her. He also repeatedly used a bell to summon her to his room for trivial reasons, sometimes just because he thought a flower was not correctly positioned in a vase.

Mrs Brown withstood all this because she knew her husband was in constant pain, but she admitted his behaviour was worsening and it was wearing her down.

While Mrs Brown had the fortitude to endure her husband's spiteful behaviour, Eric did not, and when he was interviewed by police, he was very co-operative, volunteering to give a written statement and explaining his motives. That statement was to prove pivotal in a controversial murder trial which was to follow.

On Monday September 20th, eight weeks after Archibald Brown was blown to pieces by an anti-tank mine, Eric Brown, still a few weeks away from his 20th birthday, sat quietly in the dock at Southend Police Court for a preliminary hearing. He showed no sign of emotion, despite the main exhibit in the prosecution case being on view – the twisted scorched remains of the wheelchair.

But when a police officer referred to the statement Eric made when arrested, Eric's defence counsel Mr J.P. Nolan made a dramatic intervention, challenging the admission of the statement. 'According to my instructions, my client was induced to make the statement, not only by a promise but a threat,' he told the court.

Nolan claimed that officers taking the statement had suggested to Eric Brown that they thought his mother was involved in the murder and that if Eric did not tell the truth, they could make it 'very unpleasant' for her.

The police strongly denied this and insisted that although Mrs Brown has been interviewed for almost five hours, no pressure was put on her, nor had any threats or promises been made to Eric.
The magistrates accepted this and permitted Eric's statement to be read out in the courtroom.

In the statement, Eric Brown said: 'I want to tell you the whole story. For the last four and a half years, and even before that, life has ceased to exist for my mother, it has become complete drudgery as a result of my father's treatment of her. I decided that the only real way in which my mother could lead a normal life and for my father to be released from his suffering, was for him to die mercifully. I therefore decided to cause his death which would leave him no longer in suffering. This was only decided upon a matter of a few days before his death.'

He continued: 'After nearly a fortnight of seeing exactly what my mother was forced to endure, I realised this could not be allowed to go on. Primarily for my mother's sake but also to a lesser degree for my father's sake, I placed the grenade underneath my father's chair not realising at the time that although it would kill him, just what his death would mean to me and all those near him. My father is now out of his suffering and I earnestly hope that my mother will now have a much more happy and normal life. This I declare is the only motive I had for bringing about my father's death. His death was, in truth, a great shock to me but what I did I am not afraid to answer for.'

It was as candid and clear-cut a confession as you could find, yet when Eric Brown went for trial two months later, in November at Essex Assizes and charged with murder, his lawyer J.P. Nolan entered a plea of not guilty.

The prosecution was represented by Sir Charles Doughty and the defence by Cecil Havers - the grandfather of the actor Nigel Havers. Initially, Sir Charles Doughty had little to do in proving the case against Eric Brown as the packed courtroom heard that the defence fully accepted that Archibald Brown had been deliberately killed by his son Eric, but that the defendant pleaded not guilty by reason of insanity.

His defence team therefore had to prove that either Eric at the time of the murder did not know what he was doing, or that if he did know, he was unaware that what he was doing was wrong. It was a tough challenge for the fact that he stole the anti-tank mine, altered its setting and then planted it on his father's wheelchair suggested premeditation and his failure to admit to the crime for several weeks suggested he knew what he had done was wrong.

Eric's mother gave evidence, revealing Eric had been a nervous child who could be moody and was sometimes depressed. She said he did

61

not mix well with other boys at school. She added that despite her husband's harsh treatment of Eric, she felt father and son were still on good terms.

A police inspector told the court that enquiries about Eric at Barclays Bank, where he had once worked, revealed that while Eric had seemed promising, he suffered occasional mental lapses when he would hammer his desk with his fists. Things came to a head when he admitted stealing a small amount of cash and stamps which he immediately repaid, so the bank chose not to report the matter to police but insisted he resign.

Further evidence of Eric's behaviour came from his commanding officer in the army, who said that while Eric appeared nervous and self-conscious, he did not seem abnormal and was given a good conduct assessment.

The most significant evidence came from Dr Rowland Hill, a psychiatrist and neurologist, who had examined Eric while he was being held in Chelmsford Prison. He told the court he believed Eric lived in his own fantasy world and concluded that he was in the early stages of schizophrenia. He said that while he questioned Eric, the boy would often stop in mid-sentence and daydream.

Dr Hill said when he directly asked Eric why he had killed his father, the boy couldn't provide a clear reason but did say that if, at the time of the murder, someone had been with him and told him of the consequences of what he was doing, he would not have done it. But Eric then added that he thought he had done 'God's will.'

The jury also heard that Dr Hill felt Eric had planted the bomb as if 'in a dream' adding: 'I do not think he thought it out in a deliberate way.'

Prosecuting counsel Sir Charles Doughty took issue with these conclusions but Dr Hill stood his ground, saying that if Eric had no one to take care of him, he would regard him as 'certifiably insane.'

Doughty queried this, asking: 'Could a man who is certifiable get a good character in the army over a period of nine months?'

Hill said he could, during 'a lucid period.'

'You think a lucid period would extend over nine months?' said Doughty.

'That is very common with this complaint,' Hill retorted.

At this critical point, the judge, Mr Justice Atkinson, intervened to point out that Eric Brown had admitted in his police statement that he did know what he was doing.

Dr Hill countered by saying that while Eric had made a logical statement to police, that statement was some weeks after the murder by which time his mental state could have changed.

More medical evidence followed, this time from Dr R.G.Lyster, the medical officer at Chelmsford Prison. He said he had seen Eric daily since his admission to the prison hospital and that in his view, Eric was sane. However, he did reveal that on one occasion Eric had attempted suicide by cutting his neck with a knife.

Cross-examined by defence counsel Cecil Havers, Dr Lyster said that while he thought Eric was not mentally stable, his behaviour in his view did not amount to insanity.

Dr Hill was then recalled to the witness box and told the court the attempted suicide was entirely consistent with someone suffering from schizophrenia. 'He told me he came to prison in a happy, buoyant frame of mind and that he suddenly realised for the first time that by what he had done people might call him a murderer. That had a depressing effect on him and he attempted suicide.'

Summing up, Mr Justice Atkinson told the jury: 'According to the boy's statement, he had a clear recollection of what he had done, and he gave his reasons. You have to decide whether his act was an emotional momentary impulse of which Dr Hill has spoken.'

The jury considered the matter for just 45 minutes before returning a verdict of guilty but insane.

The judge told Eric Brown he would be detained 'as a criminal lunatic' at His Majesty's pleasure - in effect a sentence of indeterminate length.

In fact, it turned out to be sentence of 32 years, for in 1975 Eric Brown was released from prison and appears to have merged anonymously back into society. I have not been able to find any record of his death, but were he still alive, would now be 98 years old.

THE SECRET TRIAL

When a man is shot dead in an English seaside town and the gunman is quickly arrested, the process of arranging a trial would seem to be straightforward. But this murder was so controversial and so sensitive, the trial had to held on a ship anchored off the coast and the verdict was never officially announced.

The circumstances which lead to this extraordinary trial appear at first glance to be relatively unremarkable yet they led to international repercussions and an impenetrable shroud of secrecy.

The event that sparked led to this trial took place in 1926, just before 11 pm on Thursday August 26th. The location was Rosherville, a suburb of Gravesend, a sizable town on the Kent coast.

As factory worker George Jenner walked home from his evening shift, he thought he heard gunshots and as he turned a corner, he saw a crowd of people running towards him, including two young women, several American sailors and various local residents. As they ran past him, Jenner saw a man lying on the pavement struggling to get up and saying he had been shot.

Jenner and a passer-by decided the man needed urgent medical attention and did not waste time calling for an ambulance – they got the injured man onto a bus and took him directly to Gravesend Hospital just a few minutes away.

Their commendable efforts proved unsuccessful for the man had a serious bullet wound to his abdomen and when surgeons operated the next morning, they found the damage was so significant, they could not save him. This was a desperately sad situation for the man was just 23 years old and had to be told he had only hours to live and that nothing could be done.

The young man was still able to talk and gave his name as Emilio Paredes, a Filipino who was a mess attendant on an American destroyer, the USS Sharkey, which was moored off Gravesend while involved in training exercises. Paredes also named the man who had shot him – Le Bon Smith, an American sailor serving on another ship, the USS Lardner, also moored offshore.

A police superintendent and a local Justice of the Peace were called to Paredes bedside and wrote down his statement. In it, the young man confirmed he knew he was dying and had no hope of recovery. He went on to explain why he had been shot, and it was a controversial development as he claimed it was a racial issue.

Paredes and other Filipino friends from his ship had come ashore in Gravesend to attend a dance at a church hall, and on arrival found a number of white American sailors also there, dancing with local English girls. The American sailors resented the presence of the Filipinos and had actually been to the church hall a few days earlier and tried to get Filipinos banned from attending the dance. 'In our country, we do not permit these people to mix with us,' one of the sailors told the church warden. But the request for a ban was refused.

Surprisingly, there was no trouble between the two factions during the dance itself but feelings were running high and it was soon after the dance ended and people were leaving that trouble erupted.

Exactly what took place was later disputed but the clearest and perhaps the most believable account came from Emilio Paredes in his deathbed statement to police: 'When I got to the dance, three American sailors by the name of Smith, Coffer and Anderson were there. I realize while I was dancing they did not like us to be mixed up with the dance as we are Filipinos. The dance closed at exactly 11 o'clock and while we were on our way to the ship these three fellows passed by me and when they were ten yards in front of me, I heard Smith fire several times and all I know, I fall down'.

Asked if he was sure it was Smith who fired the shots, Paredes said: 'I am quite sure.'

'Do you know why Smith fired at you?'

'Because he hates Filipinos.' he replied.

This claim of a racial motive was an explosive ingredient in a case which had already shocked the local community and which was to have international repercussions.

The man named by Paredes was Le Bon Smith, aged 28 and from South Carolina. He was a gunner on the USS Lardner and after the shooting incident had returned with his friends to his ship. The Kent police wanted to interview the men and sent Superintendent William Paramour and other officers to the ship to make an arrest. However, the ship's officer told the police that the men who attended the dance were already in custody on the ship and they would not be handed over. He maintained that while the alleged crime had been committed on shore and the USS Lardner was in British territorial waters, the ship itself was American territory and therefore the British authorities had no legal jurisdiction.

This was an unforeseen development and the police retreated to shore and reported the encounter to their superiors who in turn referred matter to the Home Secretary Sir William Joynson-Hicks.

Neither the American nor the British governments wanted the incident to cause a political rift so some way was sought to avoid either side losing face. It was agreed that an investigation be conducted on board the USS Sharkey, carried out by the ship's officers but with Superintendent Paramour of the Kent police permitted to attend. Also present would be Le Bon Smith, who would be represented by an officer but would not be cross-examined.

Smith's shipmate Russell Coffer, aged 28 and from Virginia, gave evidence and confirmed that he had left the church hall with Smith and Anderson and two English girls they had met at the dance, Lucy Kielty and Ivy Cole. He said that as they walked past a group of Filipinos, he was stuck on the back of the head and knocked to the ground. And said he was certain it was one of the Filipinos who struck him. He also denied owning a gun and said he had never seen Le Bon Smith with a gun.

The other sailor in the trio was Vernon Anderson, a 22-year-old from South Carolina. He too said one of the Filipinos had struck Coffer and another one tried to hit him while on the ground but he stepped forward to prevent a second blow. He said he heard two shots and saw Paredes fall, but did not know who had fired the shots. He maintained that neither he nor Smith had guns.

However, evidence from the Filipinos told a very different story. Bonifacio Barben, a cook on the Lardner, had left the dance with Paredes and three others. He said he did not see anyone hit Coffer but he did see Smith shoot Paredes and that he ran away because he thought he might be killed too.

Another Filipino, Francisco Atendido, a mess attendant on the

Sharkey, said he saw Smith take a gun from his pocket and shoot Paredes so he too ran from the scene. And another mess attendant on the Sharkey, Narcisco Gavilo, told the hearing he heard shots and identified Smith as the gunman.

Le Bon Smith heard all the allegations but did not give any evidence and the hearing was told that no gun had been found.

The delicate issue of exact jurisdiction was still under discussion between the British and US governments when news came that Emilio Paredes had died, just five days after being shot.

That same day, by coincidence or by deliberate decision, the two American ships Lardner and Sharkey sailed out of British waters and headed for Spain, taking with them the chief suspect and key witnesses.

The Home Office appeared to want an easy way out of this tricky diplomatic dilemma, for they raised no protest at the hasty departure of the two ships. Instead, the Home Secretary readily agreed to a proposal by Alanson Houghton, the US ambassador, that Smith be dealt with under US Navy court martial regulations. The Home Secretary said he took this decision 'as a matter of international courtesy' as no British citizen was directly involved.

The outcome of that court martial would prove to be a sensation in itself but before that hearing could take place, an inquest into the death of Emilio Paredes was held at Gravesend Town Hall on September 1st, though such an inquiry would be clearly hampered by the absence of vital witnesses.

The coroner's court was told it was alleged that after leaving the dance, an American sailor was struck on the head by a stone wrapped in a handkerchief and wielded by one of the group of Filipinos and that in retaliation, the American sailors had turned around and one of them fired a shot that killed Emilio Paredes.

With the none of the sailors nor the Filipinos present, the primary witnesses were the two English girls who were with the sailors - Lucy Kielty and Ivy Cole.

Lucy was a married woman whose husband was away serving with the army in India. She said that during the evening she had danced with 'white sailors, coloured sailors and civilians'. She said there were no problems between the sailors and Filipinos during the dance – 'They did not associate.'

She said that when they left the dance they walked past a group of Filipinos and one of the American sailors Coffer suddenly fell to the ground, after which she heard several shots. Despite admitting she was only two or three feet from the sailors, she insisted she had not seen anyone fire the shots.

The coroner Mr G. Evans Penman clearly found this hard to believe. 'I cannot help thinking you are keeping something back,' he told her.

She was questioned further but insisted she did not see the shooting, which drew further incredulity from the coroner. 'It seems an extraordinary thing to me that you were within three feet of the man alleged to have fired yet you did not see anything,' he said.

And if he expected a more revealing account from the other witness Ivy Cole, he was in for a disappointment. Ivy, an 18-year-old shop assistant, while admitting she was actually alongside Le Bon Smith when the shots were fired, claimed she didn't see who fired them. The coroner could barely contain his annoyance. ' You say you were within a foot of the men, one of whom is alleged to have fired the fatal shot, yet you say you saw nothing. I do not believe a word of it.'

He warned her that he was certain she had not told the whole truth and that if she committed perjury, she could be sent to prison. The warning went unheeded. Ivy Cole persisted with her account and did not vary from it.

The jury were unimpressed with the evidence of the two women and returned a verdict of wilful murder by Le Bon Smith and a warrant was then issued for his arrest and committal for trial. But it was not to be.

Governments on both sides of the Atlantic wanted to avoid the case becoming an international news story so a hasty compromise was devised which resulted in one of the most extraordinary – perhaps even unique - trials in British legal history. It would take place in a courtroom on board an American ship anchored off Gravesend and whatever the verdict, it would not be revealed!

On October 29th 1926, just three months after Emilio Parades was murdered, a court was assembled in the ward room of the USS Lardner, which had returned to British waters from its Spanish excursion. On board were Le Bon Smith, his friends Coffer and Anderson, the Filipino witnesses and Superintendent Paramour of the Kent police who had investigated the case from the outset.

As it was a US court martial, the presiding officer was Captain William Galbraith and the prosecuting officer was Lieutenant Moses Byington. Representing Le Bons Smith was the perhaps inappropriately named Lieutenant R.U. Failing.

What followed over the next few days was initially a repeat of the Gravesend coroner's inquest.

The Filipino witnesses again gave their evidence reaffirming they saw Smith fire a gun and Superintendent Paramour confirmed that he had tried to get Le Bon Smith brought ashore for questioning after Paredes named him as the shooter but was told that Smith 'could not leave the ship'.

At the conclusion of the prosecution evidence, the hearing was adjourned for the weekend and resumed on the Monday when Lieutenant Failing began to present the case for the defence. His first witness was Russell Coffer who admitted he, Anderson and Smith had tried to get the Filipinos banned from attending the dance and that one of the Filipinos had made a complaint about this to an officer. Coffer said he had then been warned about his conduct and reminded that English law was different to that of the United States. Coffer said he then discussed this with Anderson and Smith. 'We decided we would not bother any more about Filipinos,' he said. He also denied Smith had a gun on the night of the shooting.

Lucy Kielty gave evidence and was asked if she fully understood the meaning of perjury. She confirmed she did and went on to repeat her story that she did not see the shooting and did not know who had fired the shots. She was followed by Ivy Cole who not only denied seeing the shooting but this time claimed she didn't even realise there had been a shooting. She said she thought the sound of the shots was probably a motorcycle tyre bursting.

Vernon Anderson told the court that he not seen the shooting but that the Filipinos were swinging weighted handkerchiefs and were the aggressors - the sailors were just trying to keep out of their way.

Then Le Bon Smith gave evidence. He said as they walked past the Filipinos, Coffer was struck on the head and fell to pavement. Smith said he then turned to face the Filipinos but as he did so, he heard two shots and the Filipinos ran away. He said he didn't know where the shots came from and was unaware anyone had been shot until he went to the hospital with Coffer who needed his head wound treated. He said neither he, Coffer nor Anderson had carried a gun.

Summing up, the prosecuting officer Lieutenant Byington made a telling point – after the shots were fired, all the Filipinos ran away but the white sailors had not – because, he suggested, they knew there would be no more shots.

He said he thought it 'remarkable' that the sailors and the two girls had not discussed the incident after it happened and he believed Anderson and Smith knew much more about the incident than they admitted. He also pointed out that it was most unlikely that Emilio Paredes, knowing he was dying, would lie about who shot him.

Byington made a strong prosecution case and Smith's defence advocate Lieutenant Failing had little to counter it. The best he could do was to suggest the Filipinos had colluded because they hated white men.

This racial aspect has to be viewed against the racial attitudes that prevailed in Britain in the 1920s and which might perhaps explain why the two British women chose to be at best rather economical with their evidence at the inquest and at the court martial.

In the mid-1920s there were an estimated 20,000 black people in Britain and in 1919 when there was much unemployment and a housing shortage, there had been a number of race riots across the country particularly involving dock workers and sailors who felt their jobs and homes were threatened by the growing number of immigrants. Five people were killed in the riots.

Looking back at race relations at that time, Chamion Caballero, in a study published in 2019 titled Interraciality in Early Twentieth Century Britain says: 'By the 1920s, Press opinion on inter-racial relationships in Britain had moved to a tone much more aggressive and condemnatory in nature, while fictional and artistic depictions—mostly focusing on the erotic thrill of interraciality across Empire—continued to underscore the message that interraciality was an exotic 'un-British' state of affairs.'

Resentment of an increasing black presence in Britain continued to grow throughout the 1930s and into the post-war era and was particularly highlighted in 1943 when the famous Trinidadian cricketer Learie Constantine was awarded damages in the High Court after being turned away from a London hotel because the owner believed his presence would offend American servicemen staying there.

Such potentially explosive racial sensitivities and the need to maintain good relations between Britain and the USA appear to have been a factor at the court martial of Le Bon Smith because after deliberating for two hours, there was an extraordinary agreement between representatives of both sides that the verdict would not be disclosed. No explanation for this decision was given.

A few days later, the court reconvened to consider disciplinary charges against Coffer and Anderson and possibly others but the findings were kept secret.

In may seem incredible today in an age of a probing Press, freedom of information and unfettered social media that so controversial a trial was hushed up but in the pre-war era, the Press and the public were more respectful of Government authority and as neither the victim nor his alleged killer were British, the matter faded away.

Today, almost 100 years after the murder of Emilio Paredes, no official disclosure about the case or its verdict has ever been made and extensive detective work by various researchers has failed to find any records of the court martial or its decision.

However, one tiny but very significant fact was uncovered. US immigration records show that on December 30th, 1926, just two weeks after the court martial, an American ship, the SS President Van Buren, left the port of Marseilles bound for Boston. When eleven days later it arrived at the American port, official immigration records reveal that Le Bon Smith, Vernon Anderson and two Filipino men were taken from the ship and immediately transferred to Charlestown Prison.

It would seem the court martial had found Smith guilty of murder and sentenced him to an unspecified term on imprisonment, with perhaps his co-defendants given lesser sentences.

It is not known how long Smith was in prison nor what he did when he was eventually released, but it is known that he died in New York in 1951, aged 53. If between leaving prison and his death, he ever spoke about the murder, no records have been found.

This is a sad and still disturbing case of racial tensions and political sensitivities forming a barrier to a fair and open public trial, with the young murder victim Emilio Paredes becoming just a pawn in a game of diplomatic chess.

CHEATING THE HANGMAN

When a convicted murderer cheats the hangman not once but three times and then goes on to achieve celebrity status and wealth is probably unique in criminal history.

Although the murder took place in 1884 when Queen Victoria was still monarch, the man who committed the murder was released from prison in 1907 and immediately began a career of fame and fortune by cashing in on his notoriety which was so great that books and television programmes about him were still being produced more than a century later.

The celebrity killer was John Lee, born in Devon and at 16 set for a career in the Royal Navy. But then fate intervened and set him off on a path to petty crime, then murder, and eventually wealth and fame - an extraordinary journey.

That journey began when Lee caught pneumonia while a naval cadet and was invalided out of the service. Just before joining the navy, Lee had briefly worked as a servant to an elderly woman who lived in Babbacombe on the South Devon coast. Her name was Emma Keyse, a spinster of 69 who had once been a lady-in-waiting to Queen Victoria.

Miss Keyse owned a large thatched cottage located on the Babbacombe seafront, where she lived with three women servants, and when she learned that John Lee was now out of the navy and looking for work, she recommended him to a friend, Colonel Edward Brownlow in nearby Torquay.

This act of kindness was to have dire consequences.

While Lee had been a good servant for Miss Keyse before he joined the navy, his character had changed and within a few months of joining the staff at the residence of Colonel Brownlow, Lee stole some of the family silver and tried to pawn it, but he was caught, tried, convicted and sentenced to six months in prison.

Just before he was due to be released, the kindly Miss Keyse again stepped in to try to help him. On January 1st 1884 she wrote to the prison chaplain stating that she felt Lee was 'simple-minded and easily lead astray' and that as he had been honest and obedient when working for her, she was prepared to give him another chance and employ him as a gardener.

This was to prove a terrible mistake, for Miss Keyse had badly misjudged John Lee. He took advantage of her confidence in him by being lazy and often ignoring her instructions. Miss Keyse felt unable to sack him after giving him so much assistance, but she did reduce his wages by sixpence which was 20 per cent of his weekly wage.

Lee was angry at her decision and also unsettled by the fact that she was planning to sell the house, though Miss Keyse has assured him she would recommend that the new owners should retain him. Lee was unconvinced and was even more resentful. His anger came to a head just two weeks later.

In the early hours of November 15th, Miss Keyes left her bedroom and went down downstairs into the hall, perhaps having heard a noise. In the hall she was viciously attacked, her skull smashed with a heavy blow and her throat cut. Her attacker then dragged her body into the dining room, set fire to it and also started fires in other rooms in the house. Soon the smell of burning aroused the women servants who started to yell 'Fire!' and as they started to look for Miss Keyse, John Lee appeared, partly dressed as if he had just got up, and he helped them search all the rooms until they entered the dining room and found the body of their employer with burning newspapers scattered around her. Lee suggested an intruder had broken in but his acting was soon to be exposed.

A police search of the property revealed an axe, a blood-stained knife and tin of paraffin which had been used to start the fires. Some of the items were found in or near a small pantry where Lee slept on a camp-bed, along with a pair of his trousers which were heavily blood-stained. Lee still claimed the fire and the murder were the work of an intruder though when it was put to him that the intruder would have had to have climbed over him on his camp-bed to get at the knife and the tin of paraffin, Lee had no credible answer.

At his trial, he pleaded not guilty, still maintaining the crimes were carried out by an intruder but after hearing the evidence, the jury took only 40 minutes to find him guilty. The judge told him the crime was 'as barbarous as was ever committed' and sentenced him to be hanged.

Lee took the sentence so calmly, the judge commented on it and Lee told him: 'The reason I am calm and collected is that I trust in my Lord, and He knows I am innocent.' The extraordinary events which were to follow were, according to John Lee, the result of Divine Intervention.

At 8am on February 23rd 1885 Lee stood on the scaffold at Exeter Prison with a noose around his neck and white hood over his head, with hangman James Berry ready to proceed. After the chaplain had conducted a short service, Berry pulled the lever to open the trapdoor and drop Lee to his fate.

But nothing happened. The trapdoor didn't open and despite Berry jerking the lever again and warders running forward to stamp on the trapdoor, it still wouldn't open. Lee was moved aside and the trapdoor and its mechanism checked but no fault was found so Lee was stood on the boards again and Berry pulled the level. Again, the trapdoor failed to open.

This time, not only was the mechanism re-examined but warders trimmed wood from the edges of the trapdoor to ensure no part of it touched the frame. Lee was led to the trapdoor for a third time but inexplicably and some might say miraculously, it again failed to spring open.

The hangman, the warders and the witnesses were badly shaken by events and this time, Lee was taken back to his cell while a carpenter was called to overall the trapdoor. A fourth attempt to hang John Lee was imminent but the chaplain refused to take part and so did the prison surgeon who said Lee had suffered enough. Without a chaplain, the hanging could not take place so the matter was reported to the Home Secretary Sir William Harcourt who ruled that the death sentence should be commuted to life imprisonment. His hand may have been hastened by a communication from none other than Queen Victoria herself, saying it would be 'too cruel' to execute Lee after all that had happened, adding: 'Imprisonment for life seems the only alternative.'

After hearing news of his sentence, Lee sent a letter to his sister in which he said it was 'the Lord's will' that he had been spared.

While that may be true, an official investigation to discover why the trapdoor jammed found that a metal hinge was mis-aligned and while the trapdoor worked perfectly in tests when there was no weight on it, it would jam with the extra weight of a body.

That should really have been the end of this remarkable case but it was to create world-wide publicity again when John Lee was released from prison 22 years later, in 1907. Lee may not have been too intelligent in the way he committed murder, but he was smart enough to realise that now he was free from prison, he could cash in on his fame as The Man They Couldn't Hang.

He immediately wrote his autobiography and received £240 (about £28,000 in today's money) for it to be serialised in a popular national magazine. In the autobiography, Lee gave his version of the murder, still denying he was responsible and saying how shocked he was when finding the body of Miss Keyse, describing her as 'my poor dear mistress'.

The publicity from the magazine gave him instant celebrity status, allowing him to charge large fees for personal appearances, billed as 'John 'Babbacombe' Lee - The Man They Couldn't Hang'. He was also paid substantial sums to relate his life story in pubs and at fairgrounds, giving vivid accounts of the night of the murder and of his ordeal during the attempts to hang him. These appearances attracted thousands of people.

A silent film called The Man They Couldn't Hang was made in 1912 but not screened, though in 1921 a re-edited and longer version of it was released and shown at cinemas across Britain, attracting huge audiences. The film added to Lee's fame and notoriety.

However, in 1911, four years after his release from prison, Lee – by now quite wealthy - was aware that many people were disgusted at him still cashing in on such a brutal murder and sensing public opinion was turning, he decided he would leave Britain for a new life abroad, where it would be easier to keep a low profile. His destination was initially a matter of speculation, some saying he was in Australia, others in Canada or America. However, it is known that Lee and a woman called Adelina Gibbs, who he had met in a London pub, sailed for New York in 1911 after which little was heard of them. They eventually settled in Milwaukee, merging into the local community without anyone knowing of Lee's murderous past.

However, thanks to relentless detective work by Mike Holgate and Ian David Waugh, authors of The Man They Couldn't Hang, (Sutton

Publishing, 2005) it was established that Lee and Adelina remained in Milwaukee and had a daughter Evelyn, who was killed in an accident aged 19. And by changing his first name from John to James and also switching addresses, Lee's sensational background never came to the attention of the US authorities or journalists. He was able to lead a quiet family life until he died of a heart condition in Milwaukee in March 1945 at the age of 80.

John Lee may be long gone but he is certainly not forgotten. Many books and magazine features have since been written about him, the case has featured on television and there has even been a musical account of his life courtesy of the folk-rock band Fairport Convention, who in 1971 released an album called Babbacombe Lee, recounting in song the life and times of The Man They Couldn't Hang.

THE SEDUCTIVE WIFE

Police officers called to a house in suburban Bournemouth found architect Francis Rattenbury slumped in an armchair, near to death with severe head injuries. His wife Alma was beside him and she told police: 'I did it with a mallet. I'd have shot him if I'd had a gun.'

When a few days later the man died of his injuries, his wife made a formal statement again admitting she had attacked and killed her husband, so it was no surprise that Alma Rattenbury was charged with murder.

Just one thing was wrong with that rather conclusive set of events – Alma Rattenbury had not murdered her husband. She was not even in the room when he was brutally battered. So why had she been so keen to confess to a crime which at that time still carried the death penalty?

The start of this extraordinary murder case began in September 1934 when an advertisement was placed in a Bournemouth newspaper seeking 'a willing lad, 14-18, for house work.'

The advertisement was placed by Alma Rattenbury, a 38-year-old middle-class housewife living in Manor Road, Bournemouth with her much-respected husband Francis, an award-winning architect who had designed the parliament buildings in Victoria, capital of British Columbia.

Francis Rattenbury was 30 years older than his wife and the couple had met in Canada a decade earlier when he was a celebrated architect and she was a young glamorous pianist who gave recitals and also wrote popular songs for dance bands and which were often played on BBC radio.

Alma was very attractive and was never short of admirers. Even when in her twenties she had already been married twice. She was giving a recital in a hotel in British Columbia when Francis Rattenbury first saw her. He was instantly captivated, especially after Alma came up to him and told him: 'You have a lovely face. It is the kindest face I ever saw.'

It seemed to be a genuine instance of love at first sight, and as their relationship developed, Rattenbury divorced his wife and Alma divorced her husband. The lovestruck couple then married, and in

81

1925 moved to England, settling in Bournemouth, where they lived happily together for several years and had a son called John.

But by the early 1930s, cracks were beginning to appear in the marriage. Francis, now in his late 60s, had become rather dull, had business worries, was drinking heavily, suffered bouts of depression and the couple no longer shared a bedroom. Alma, still in her late 30s, was bored and disillusioned with the dreary life she now had with her once distinguished and celebrated husband. She was also sexually frustrated.

Events took a fateful turn when Alma placed a newspaper advertisement for a handyman to work at the Rattenbury residence. One applicant was handsome 18-year-old George Stoner, who could not only help with household duties but was also able to drive. He was given the job as chauffeur and handyman and his duties quickly extended when Alma Rattenbury made it clear to him that he was very welcome in her bedroom. Within a week of his starting his new job, she had cornered Stoner in the conservatory, kissed him passionately and to ensure he got the message tore open her blouse to reveal bare breasts.

A passionate affair began with Stoner sharing her bed most nights. Her bedroom was conveniently located on the ground floor, well away from her husband's upstairs bedroom.

Whether Francis Rattenbury was ignorant of the affair or just chose to ignore it isn't certain, but either way, the eventual outcome was to be both sensational and tragic.

Stoner was a working-class lad with little experience of life or women, and quickly became besotted with the sophisticated and worldly Alma, who had bought him expensive new clothes and had even taken him to spend a few days with her in a smart London hotel.

Obsessed with Alma, Stoner became very possessive and also very jealous of her ailing husband, who he wrongly suspected still might be having occasional sex with Alma. This jealousy reached a peak when Stoner learned that Francis Rattenbury was planning to go to Bridport for a meeting with a business associate and wanted Alma to accompany him. They had been invited to stay overnight and though Alma had assured Stoner she and her husband would be staying in separate rooms while away, the young chauffeur was furious about the arrangement.

Later that evening, Stoner came into Alma's bedroom looking agitated and told her she would not be going to Bridport the next day because he had just attacked and injured her husband. Alma then heard Francis Rattenbury groaning and she ran from her ground-floor bedroom into the adjacent living room where she saw her husband slumped in an armchair, unconscious and bleeding from the head. Stoner admitted he had hit him with a wooden mallet which he had hidden in the garden.

Alma became hysterical and screamed for her live-in maid Irene Riggs to call the doctor. They then wrapped a towel around Rattenbury's head and with the help of Stoner, they moved him to his bedroom. Soon doctor William O'Donnell arrived and after examining Rattenbury's head wounds, called a local surgeon to the scene.

The two doctors arranged for Rattenbury to be taken to a nearby nursing home for a more detailed assessment. There they found three severe wounds which they knew could not have been self-inflicted, so they immediately notified the police.

First to arrive was Constable Arthur Bagwell, who found Alma Rattenbury excited, very drunk, talking incoherently, laughing and even playing records on the gramophone. She danced around and a one point tried to kiss the policeman. She also told the officer: 'I did it with a mallet. He has lived too long.'

A little later when a police inspector arrived, she was just as candid: 'I'll tell you in the morning where the mallet is,' she said. 'I shall make a better job of it next time. I made a proper muddle of it. I thought I was strong enough.'

By now it was 4 am and Doctor O'Donnell had returned. He gave Alma half a grain of morphia to calm her and put her to bed. She slept for a few hours and soon after 8am, the police decided she was fit enough to make a formal statement. In it she said she and her husband had been playing cards together when he dared her to kill him, telling her she 'hadn't got the guts to do it'. She said she fetched a mallet and hit him on the head.

Police decided to take her to Bournemouth police station. As she left the house, Alma told Irene Riggs and Stoner: 'Don't make fools of yourselves.' Her young son John who had been in the house the whole time but who knew nothing of what had taken place, watched her leaving.

At the police station, Alma was formally charged with causing grievous bodily harm with intent to murder – at this stage Francis Rattenbury was still alive but had not regained consciousness.

When charged, Alma said: 'That's right. I did it deliberately and I'd do it again.'

Later that morning she made a brief appearance in the magistrates' court where on the advice of her solicitor, she entered a plea of not guilty. She appeared dazed and bewildered and was taken to Holloway Prison.

Next day George Stoner, while alone with housemaid Irene Riggs, told her it was he who had attacked Francis Rattenbury, using a mallet he had borrowed from his grandparents. This was a shock to Irene, who until then was convinced Alma had committed the crime. But Irene realised that while Stoner had confessed to her, that might not be sufficient evidence as later he could deny what he had said. She was uncertain what to do, so did nothing.

The following day Stoner received a letter from Alma which she had sent from her prison cell. Stoner began drinking heavily and shouted: 'Mrs Rattenbury is in jail and I put her there.'

The situation worsened next day when news came out that Francis Rattenbury had died of his injuries. Irene Rigg was in turmoil and when by chance Doctor O'Donnell called at the house, she told him of Stoner's confession and he immediately rang the police. They quickly arrested Stoner and charged him with murder.

Stoner seemed eager to admit his guilt. He quickly told police Mrs Rattenbury had nothing to do with the attack on her husband, that he alone had struck the fatal blows after being incensed with jealousy. He said had watched through the French windows as Alma had given her husband a goodnight kiss. 'I waited, and crept into through the French windows which were unlocked. I think he must have been asleep when I hit him.'

He added: 'There should be a doctor with her when they tell her I have been arrested because she will go out of her mind.'

Despite Stoner's confession, police still maintained a charge of murder against Alma Rattenbury and she and Stoner were committed for trial at the Old Bailey. While awaiting trial, Alma wrote a song for George Stoner. One of the lines was: 'By some mistake you filled my empty days but now I wake to face the parting ways.' Another line said: 'I seem to climb to heaven in loving you.'

Awaiting trial, Alma was still insisting that she alone had killed her husband and intended to change her plea to guilty, ignoring advice from her lawyers and even from the prison governor, who believed she was innocent. Eventually, Alma was persuaded that there was nothing she could do to help Stoner and that unless she told the truth, she would hang with him.

Alma had two children - one with Rattenbury and one from a previous marriage who was living with a relative – and a breakthrough came when it was pointed out to her that it was not fair to her children to grow up branded as the children of a murderer. She then agreed to plead not guilty.

When the trial opened on May 27th 1935 the Press were clamouring to get seats in the courtroom. The case had made sensational headlines in Britain and internationally for weeks – a respectable older woman having a torrid affair with her young chauffeur which led murder was the perfect scandal for the popular newspapers. Demand to be in court was so intense that people at the head of the queue were selling their places to others further back.

The Daily Mirror described Alma as 'more than a pretty woman... her face is attractive with large perfect eyes. She wears a dark blue coat and hat with gloves to match with a certain chic.'

Stoner was described as looking younger than his 18 years and had 'a gentle face.'

Opening for the prosecution, Mr Reginald Croom-Johnson set out to establish that the murder of Francis Rattenbury was a joint venture between his wife and her lover who both wanted him out of the way. He said that while Stoner had fetched the mallet, either of them could have struck the blows.

A crucial part of the prosecution's evidence were the clear admissions of guilt by Alma when police had arrived at the scene, and later her further statement of guilt at the police station. However, this was rather undermined by Dr O'Donnell who in evidence said she was not only drunk at the time but he had also injected her with morphia.

Asked if Alma would have been fit to make a statement to police the next morning, O'Donnell was definite: 'I should not place any credence on any statement given under such circumstances,' he said.

His evidence was backed up by a written report from the governor of Holloway prison who said Alma was 'very depressed and seemed confused' when she arrived at the prison.

Then Alma gave evidence which lasted three hours. She was composed throughout, even when under cross-examination she was forced to give the most intimate details of her passionate affair with George Stoner. But when it came to the actual murder, said she had no recollection of anything that happened after putting a towel around her husband's head and then drinking a lot of whisky to 'block out the picture.' She said she had no memory of saying anything to the police.

All this put Stoner's own defence lawyer Joshua Casswell in great difficulty. He had been instructed by Stoner to not say anything at all which might reflect badly on Alma, who he still loved deeply. So Casswell could not put her under any pressure in the witness box and neither did he call Stoner to give evidence.

Recalling the case at a later date, Casswell said: 'I was unable to cross-examine Mrs Rattenbury at all strongly. If I had done so, Stoner was quite capable of interrupting me from the dock with a cry that I had got it all wrong and he was the murderer.'

On the fifth day of the trial, the jury retired to consider its verdicts and took less than an hour to make their decisions. Alma Rattenbury was found not guilty of the murder of her husband but George Stoner was found guilty and sentenced to hang.

Soon after the sentencing, Stoner told his father: 'I am content. They have set her free. Whatever happens to me does not matter.'

Alma was distraught and had to be moved to a London nursing home after her house was besieged by reporters. She gave instructions that every effort should be made to help Stoner regardless of cost and she made several applications to see him in prison but she was refused permission.

Just a few days after the verdicts, Alma took a train from London to Bournemouth, but got off at Christchurch. She walked across a meadow and sat down on the bank of the river and began writing a note on an envelope. In the note, she said: 'I tried this morning to throw myself under a train at Oxford Circus. Too many people about. Then a bus – still too many people about. One must be bold to do a thing like this. It is beautiful here and I am alone. Thank God for peace at last.'

She then calmly walked waist-deep into the river and stabbed herself several time in the chest with a knife. She was seen in the river by a passing farmworker who tried to save her but he couldn't swim and was unable to reach her in mid-stream.

When the news of Alma's suicide was given to Stoner, he broke down and wept.

Despite the brutality of the attack on Francis Rattenbury, public sympathy for Stoner was growing – many thought he was a naïve young man caught up in a situation he didn't know how to handle.
A petition to appeal the death sentence gathered more than 300,000 signatures and an appeal was granted. Stoner's defence counsel Joshua Casswell claimed Stoner had misled his lawyers about his role in the murder because he did not wish to incriminate Alma Rattenbury and that the two defendants should have been tried separately. But the Lord Chief Justice quickly dismissed the appeal as 'a mere waste of time.'

However, the next day the Home Secretary commuted Stoner's death sentence to life imprisonment. Stoner was a model prisoner and got early release after serving only seven years. Freed in 1942 and still only 26 years old, Stoner joined the army and took part in the D-Day landing. Later he married and continued to live in the Bournemouth area, dying in 2000 at the age of 83.

This bizarre murder case is one of the most tragic of its kind, and with an outcome that may possibly be unique – a woman who did not commit murder takes her own life while the man who did commit murder went on to start a new life.

Postscript: Both the young sons of Alma Rattenbury went on to marry and have successful business careers.

The younger one John was in the house on the night of the murder. He was aged six. In an interview in 1977 he recalled the tragedy. 'No one would tell me what had happened but I had a feeling it was something terrible,' he said.

It was a year later before a boy at school told him what had really happened to his parents. 'It was such a shock – I had been told they were on vacation,' he said.

John Rattenbury also revealed how he felt about George Stoner who had not only killed his father but in effect had driven his mother to suicide. 'I never felt any animosity towards him, ' he said.
'He was so young and so impressionable. I just felt he was a terrible victim of circumstance. I'm sure that he suffered great guilt.'

THE MYSTERY MAN

If a man with no close family or friends moves into a new area and soon after just disappears, it is natural for the few who encountered him at his new location to assume he has probably returned to wherever he came from.

That is exactly what happened when 57-year-old Vivian Messiter, a quiet and rather reticent man, moved into lodging in Southampton in September 1928 and set up a small business nearby in a lock-up garage and storeroom. Yet only six weeks after he arrived in Southampton, he vanished, though initially no one was really concerned.

Messiter had been born in Somerset and had served with distinction in the first world war, reaching the rank of captain before being discharged on medical grounds after being shot in both legs. He had then gone abroad for about ten years, working mainly in America and Mexico before returning to England.

He had told his landlord in Southampton that he had recently returned from abroad and was trying to set up a local sales agency for an oil company. On the morning of October 30th Messiter left his lodging saying he was going to his garage, but when he never returned, his landlord went to the premises and found them locked up. Knowing Messiter had only been in Southampton a few weeks and was struggling to get the business established, the landlord assumed he had given up and left the area.

The Wolf's Head Oil Company, for which Messiter was a regional sales agent, wondered why they hadn't heard from him for some weeks, and wrote to the garage address in Grove Street several times. When they got no response, they eventually contacted the police who sent an officer to the premises who checked and found the building secure and with no sign of a break-in. So the police also assumed Messiter had left the area and as there were no known relatives to contact, made no further inquiries. The oil company took the same view and set about appointing a new agent.

That new agent arrived on January 10th 1929, some nine weeks after Messiter had disappeared, and when he opened up the garage by forcing a padlock, he started to look around. The first thing that drew his attention was Messiter's Morris Oxford car, loaded with five cases of oil as if ready do a delivery. He then started to explore further and made an horrific discovery.

Behind some packing cases, Messiter lay dead on the floor with a terrible injury to his left eye and his skull shattered. The body has been there for weeks, decomposing and bitten by rats. The police were called and an exhaustive search of the crime scene took place, but with the long lapse of time since the murder, no witnesses and no obvious clues, they faced a tough task and so sought help from Scotland Yard, who sent a chief inspector and an inspector to assist. They examined an order book which was in Messiter's car and found a copy of a receipt for the sale of oil to an H.F.Galton. Significantly it was dated October 30th - the day Messiter disappeared.

Galton lived locally and was quickly found. He readily admitted Messiter had paid him a small commission of half a crown (about £8 in today's money) for getting him an order for oil. But he was adamant that he had never been to the Grove Street garage, claiming Messiter came to his home to make the payment. Subsequent enquiries proved that Galton was telling the truth - on the day and probable time of Messiter's murder, he was at work on Southern Railways and this was confirmed by several witnesses.

That might have been the end of a potential lead but Galton happened to mention that although the duplicate receipt was dated October 30th, Messiter had given it to him the previous day, the 29th, when he called at his house to pay him the commission. Galton said Messiter dated it for the next day because that was when the oil would be delivered. This seemed a little odd so police began to examine the duplicate receipts books more closely and were able to discover that the date on the Galton receipt had been altered, and that many other receipts were false – the names and addresses of the customers did not exist.

This pointed to someone giving fake orders to Messiter to gain commission, for police enquiries had revealed Messiter was so desperate for new orders he would pay commission in advance to sub-agents, ahead of receiving full payment from the client.

The police now began to form a theory of what probably happened on the day of the murder. They surmised that Messiter had discovered the fraud and had then confronted the suspected culprit at the garage and was fatally attacked. But who was the mystery man?

There were no other significant clues in the garage order book and other paperwork although it was noted that several of the fake commission receipts were signed WFT. Police then conducted another intensive search of the garage and made a significant discovery – a crumpled ball of paper on the floor which when opened was a note from Messiter to a W. F. Thomas confirming an appointment to meet at the garage, though it was undated. And at Messiter's lodging, police found a letter from someone applying for a job as a sales assistant which Messiter had advertised in a local newspaper. The applicant was W.F Thomas who gave an address in Cranberry Avenue, Southampton. The WFT on the forged receipts seemed certain to be W. F. Thomas. But just who was he, and even more importantly, where was he?

The search of the garage also revealed another significant find – the murder weapon. How it was overlooked in the previous searches suggests police officers were not as thorough as they could been. Behind some stacked oil drums and packing cases was a hefty hammer with a square face at one end and a sharp wedge-shaped face at the other. It was heavily blood-stained and later forensic tests revealed hairs which matched those of Vivian Messiter.

The hammer confirmed the police theory that Messiter was attacked when confronting someone about the fraudulent orders and was brutally slain to silence him.

Police made a visit to the Southampton lodging where W.F.Thomas had stayed with his mistress Lily Hambleton from October 20th to November 3rd but the couple had already left, so a nationwide search to find Thomas was launched and almost immediately Wiltshire police were in touch to say they were looking for a motor mechanic called W.F. Thomas who had very recently stolen wage packets totalling £143 (about £9,000 in today's money) from the garage where he worked.

Enquiries later revealed that while the mysterious Thomas was at the Southampton lodgings, he had gone to Downton in Wiltshire in response to an advertisement he had seen for a motor mechanic, and he was given the job. He had then returned to Southampton, and just four days after Messiter was murdered, he and Lily left their lodging leaving a false forwarding address and went straight to Downton where Thomas started his new job.

He worked there for just over three weeks but by then, perhaps realising a net might be closing around him, Thomas decided to move on again, this time to the Midlands, financed by the theft of wages from his new employer. In fact, when the wages were stolen, Thomas was still at the garage and was actually questioned by police about the theft but his smooth talking and confident manner allayed suspicions though police did tell him they would need to also make some checks with his previous employer in Southampton. Thomas had given the officers a false address for the reference and he knew that when they checked it, the game would be up. As soon as the police left, Thomas and Lily fled without even going back to their lodging.

When it became clear Thomas had lied, the police decided it was still worth searching his lodging in Downton and it turned out to be a wise decision. Behind a stove they found a scrap of paper which had the words Podmore and Manchester written on it. Manchester police were then contacted and it was revealed that they were searching for a 28-year-old motor mechanic called William Podmore who was wanted for questioning over a series of frauds involving motor vehicles. They thought Thomas and Podmore could be the same man.

Then Staffordshire police got in touch with the murder investigation officers, saying they thought the description of Thomas which had been widely circulated fitted that of a man known to them - William Podmore, a petty thief and fraudster who was from Stoke on Trent.

Police quickly rushed to his last known address but again he had moved on, though they did trace his girlfriend Lily Hambleton to an address in Stoke on Trent and she quickly confirmed Podmore had left there only hours earlier having seen newspaper reports of the Messiter murder. Lily said Podmore was on his way to Southampton to voluntarily be interviewed by the police, but was going via London and was probably staying at The Leicester Hotel in Vauxhall Bridge Road where they had stayed previously. Police raided the hotel and found Podmore, who said: 'I know what you want me for but I can explain everything.'

He was taken to Southampton police station where he proved to be a very confident and arrogant character and a very convincing liar. He admitted that he was at Messiter's garage on the morning of October 30th and said he saw Messiter talking with another sales agent who he thought was called Maxton or Baxton, who he had seen at the garage a few days earlier. Podmore said Messiter asked him to look at a magneto problem on his Morris car, and then left with the other man.

Podmore said he stayed on to repair the car and admitted he had actually used Messiter's car to go to Downton for his job interview, claiming Messiter had given him permission to give the car a good test run. He said he had returned the car later that day, parking it in the garage and then locking up. He said there was no sign of Messiter. It was a plausible tale but the police knew there was no supporting evidence that the man he claimed to have seen at the garage with Messiter earlier that day actually existed. However, there was no forensic evidence or witness evidence to charge Podmore with Messiter's murder though there was plenty of evidence to convict him of previous fraud offences in Manchester and he was sentenced to three months in prison. On his release, he was immediately arrested at the prison gates in connection with the wages theft in Wiltshire, and he was convicted and sentenced to a further six months in prison.

While Podmore was serving his sentence, police were trying to link him to the murder of Vivian Messiter, and although the evidence they had was almost wholly circumstantial, a breakthrough came when two prisoners serving time with Podmore claimed he had admitted murdering Messiter. So Podmore was then charged with murder.

The trial began in March 1930, five months after Messiter was murdered. The prosecution could produce no witnesses who saw Podmore at the garage, no forensic evidence that put him at the scene of the crime, and there were no items known to have been stolen from Messiter found in his possession. The turning point in the trial was the rather dubious testimony of two men who were in prison with Podmore. One claimed Podmore had admitted to stealing money from Messiter, the other that Podmore had actually confessed to the murder. Cross-examination by Podmore's defence counsel Herbert du Parcq – later to be made a judge and a Law Lord - showed the evidence given by both men was riddled with inconsistencies and inaccuracies.

Despite this, and a valiant closing defence speech by Mr du Parcq, at the end of the six-day trial the jury found William Podmore guilty of murder and he was sentenced to death. As he stood in the dock in a smart blue suit with a coloured handkerchief showing in the top pocket, Podmore looked shocked at the verdict and the sentence and told the judge: 'I still repeat I know nothing whatsoever about it.'

An appeal was launched because some of the police evidence had included various notations from memorandum and duplicate books found in Messiter's car. Podmore's lawyers claimed this evidence was inadmissible under a law which stated that paperwork from a deceased person could not be used unless it could be proved the writing was made 'in pursuance of a duty to his employers'. The appeal judges rejected this argument, and also rejected a claim that the trial judge had not properly summed up the defence case to the jury.

However, some public disquiet was growing about Podmore's conviction given there was no direct evidence that connected him to the crime. A petition calling for the conviction to be declared unsafe was signed by more than 12,000 people, including 79 Members Of Parliament, but it was ignored. In a final effort to save Podmore from the gallows, his lawyers tried a direct appeal to the House Of Lords but this also failed.

Six weeks later on April 22nd 1930, William Podmore was hanged at Winchester prison. He still protested his innocence and claimed the mystery man he had seen with Messiter at the garage was the murderer.

Podmore was convicted in a most extraordinary case which lacked witnesses and forensic evidence and relied heavily on conjecture as to what had actually happened on the day Vivian Messiter was brutally murdered. The verdict left many feeling that Podmore's long career as a fraudster and his brash and arrogant manner had probably done as much to ensure his conviction as the rather meagre evidence put before the court.

If there was a mystery man who murdered Vivian Messiter, he was certainly never caught.

THE BODY IN THE TRUNK

A railway porter working at Brighton station on a hot June day in 1934 became aware of a nasty smell which had been lingering in the left-luggage office for several days and was becoming increasingly unpleasant.

He traced the source of the smell to a large trunk which had been deposited two weeks earlier and when he opened the trunk to investigate, he found a large package wrapped in brown paper and tied with cord. Opening the package, the porter was shocked to find it contained the decomposing torso of a woman. A smaller package contained two hands, but the arms, legs and head were missing.

The police quickly set about trying to identify the body and put out an alert to all railway stations across the UK to check unclaimed trunks and within 24 hours, at Kings Cross station in London, another trunk was found containing two legs and two severed feet.

The police investigation was severely hampered by the absence of the woman's head and also by the fact that there was no record at either railway station of who had deposited the trunks.

The famous pathologist Sir Bernard Spilsbury was called in and he was able to establish that the victim was a woman in her late twenties, about five feet two inches tall, weighing about eight stones seven pounds and was probably from a middle-class background as her hands and nails were well-kept and showed no sign of any manual work. She was also five months pregnant.

Despite newspaper appeals and hundreds of missing person files being examined, the woman was not identified and with no other leads to follow up, the police investigation was faltering.

While murder itself is not uncommon, disposing of a body using a large trunk is quite rare. So it came as a seismic shock to the police searching for the missing body parts from the Brighton station victim when a second body in a trunk was discovered in the town.

Brighton is a gem of the English south coast, popular from the early 19th century as a stylish resort frequented by the wealthy including the Prince Regent. By the 1930s it had lost some its grandeur but was still a popular destination for Londoners taking a day trip or a long weekend – including criminals who saw holidaymakers as easy targets.

I worked in Brighton as a journalist in the 1970s and recall that once you left the elegant seafront, Brighton looked like any other town in the UK, a meld of neat suburban avenues and a network of grimy streets of shabby terraced houses.

And it was in one of these rundown back streets that a month after that first gruesome discovery of a headless body in a trunk, a painter decorating number 52 Kemp Street - an unoccupied rental property - informed police of a horrible smell coming from a large truck in one of the rooms. He didn't open the trunk but waited for the police to arrive. They removed the trunk to the police station and when they opened it, inside they found the entire body of a woman who had died from severe head injuries.

When the news broke of a second body in a trunk, there were sensational headlines locally and nationally which increased pressure on the Brighton police to track down what was widely thought to be a double-killer.

The owners of the Kemp Street house told police the previous occupant was a man called Tony Mancini who had recently moved out and not left a forwarding address. The police already knew of Mancini - he was a 26-year-old waiter, womaniser and petty criminal who used a variety of aliases. The victim was quickly identified as Violet Kaye who had been living with Tony Mancini at an address in Park Crescent, Brighton just a few weeks earlier. Violet was a former professional dancer but now aged 43 was finding stage-work hard to get and was supplementing her income with part-time prostitution.

The name of Violet Kaye had been in the missing person files examined by detectives when they were seeking clues for the first trunk murder - she had been reported missing by relatives. Tony Mancini had already been interviewed by police about Violet's disappearance but he told officers that Violet had left him after a row and he had no idea where she was. As the dismembered body found in the trunk at Brighton station was that of a much younger woman than Violet, the police saw no reason to detain Mancini and moved on to other enquiries.

Now the police wanted to re-interview him but he had already left

Brighton on a train bound for London. As Mancini used various false names including Antoni Pirillie and Jack Notyre, the police knew tracking him down was not going to be easy but a chance breakthrough came very soon. Two police officers on routine patrol on a main road near Sidcup in Kent saw a man walking along in the early hours of the morning. They stopped him for an identity check, established he was Mancini and he was quickly taken back to Brighton for questioning.

Mancini readily admitted putting Violet Kaye's body in the trunk, but denied he had killed her. He said he had returned to the basement flat they shared in Park Crescent to find her dead – perhaps murdered by one of her clients. He said he panicked because he was known to the police and thought he would be accused of killing her, so he put Violet's body in a trunk and kept it in the house for a week. When he decided to move to the Kemp Street address, he took the trunk with him where it remained for several more weeks before he left that address.

While extensive police inquiries produced no evidence at all to link Mancini to the first trunk murder, they were certain that they had a cast-iron case against Mancini for the murder of Violet Kaye so he was formally charged, and a few months later his trial began at Lewes Assizes.

Tony Mancini's leading defence counsel was Norman Birkett, widely regarded for his skills in cross-examination and for his persuasive closing speeches to juries. However, the prosecution team were certain that no amount of dazzling advocacy could overcome their overwhelming evidence.

Prosecution witnesses included a man who testified he had helped Mancini take the heavy trunk to the Kemp Street address. Another witness was a handwriting expert who said that a telegram supposedly sent by Violet Kaye to her sister, saying she was going to work abroad, was a fake – it was actually in Mancini's handwriting. And another witness – a waitress who knew Mancini well - told the court she had seen him arguing with Violet in a local cafe and that the next day, he gave her some of Violet's clothing saying she had left him and wouldn't need them anymore. The case against Mancini was steadily building up.

In cross-examination, defence counsel Norman Birkett initially concentrated on the forensic evidence. A Home Office analyst had testified that it was not possible to link blood stains found on Mancini's clothing to Violet Kaye as her body was too decomposed to get a sample of her blood. Then under Birkett's robust questioning the analyst conceded that blood stains found on Mancini's clothing could have come from him cutting himself. Then Birkett played an ace card – he introduced evidence to show that Mancini's blood-stained trousers had not been purchased until after Violet's death, so could not have been stained with her blood.

Then Birkett set to work on the eminent pathologist Sir Bernard Spilsbury, famed for providing vital forensic evidence in many high-profile murder cases over the previous 25 years - including that of the notorious Dr Crippen.

Spilsbury, who was very experienced in giving evidence and being cross-examined, stated that he thought the murder weapon was a hammer. Birkett put it to him that as Violet Kaye was known to be a heavy drinker and take morphine, it was possible she could have fallen downstairs and hit her head, causing a fatal injury. Spilsbury maintained his view that a hammer had caused the head injuries, but under relentless questioning by Birkett, was forced to concede that a fall could not be entirely ruled out.

The jury had seen the evidence of two forensic experts systematically dismantled by Birkett, who had also extracted a significant admission from Chief Inspector Robert Donaldson of Scotland Yard, who had been drafted in to assist Brighton police. Donaldson had to concede that despite extensive enquiries, the police had found no connection whatsoever between Mancini and the earlier trunk murder and that sensational Press reports linking Mancini to that crime and other crimes of violence were totally false.

Then into the witness box came Tony Mancini, who confirmed that his real name was actually Cecil England. He was clutching a rosary, seemed calm and self-assured and was eager to put his version of events before the jury. He admitted he worked as a waiter but also lived off some of the money Violet Kaye earned from prostitution. He said that when he arrived at the Kemp Street address one evening, he found the door locked so had climbed in through a window and found Violet lying on the bed. At first, he thought she was asleep but when he touched her, she was cold and he then saw blood on her pillow. He said he thought she had been killed by one of her clients.

Asked why he didn't call the police, he said; 'I considered that a man who has been convicted never gets a fair and square deal from the police.' He insisted he had just panicked, put the body in a trunk and had then sent the forged letter to Violet's sister saying she had gone away. But he was steadfast in saying he did not kill her.

Norman Birkett emphasised this to the jury, saying that while his client was 'idle, worthless, a man without morals or principles, he was not a murderer'. He suggested that Violet, while under the influence of drink and drugs, had probably sustained her head injuries after falling down the stairs.

In a powerful and eloquent closing speech, Birkett took an hour to pick holes in the prosecution case and build up a picture of Mancini as a man who got on well with Violet and had no reason to kill her, especially as her earnings as a prostitute helped support him.

In his final words to the jury, Birkett told them: 'Now that the whole matter is before you, I think I am entitled to claim for this man a verdict of not guilty, and in returning that verdict you will vindicate a principle of law – that people are not tried by newspapers, not tried by rumour, but are tried by juries called to do justice and to decide upon the evidence.' Pausing briefly for dramatic effect, he added: ' Stand firm.'

The jury considered the case for two and a half hours, and then returned a verdict of not guilty.

It was a triumph for Birkett though he later admitted the verdict gave him 'very little pleasure'. He described Mancini as 'a despicable and worthless creature.'

The police were bitterly disappointed at the verdict and while they continued investigations for some months into the death of Violet Kaye and that of the anonymous victim of the first trunk murder, no one was ever charged and the cases gradually faded from public memory.

Yet 42 years later, in 1976, the case of Violet Kaye was once again splashed across the front pages of national newspapers. Tony Mancini, by then 68 and living in obscurity, was tracked down to an address in the north of England by Alan Hart, an inquisitive News Of The World reporter. Mancini agreed to be interviewed about the trunk murder and in an astonishing development, he told Hart: 'Before I die,

I want to set the record straight. I did kill Violet Kaye.'

He added: 'When I gave evidence, I had carefully rehearsed my lines like an actor. I had practised how I should hold my hands and when I should let the tears roll down my cheeks. It might sound cold and calculating but you have to remember my life was at stake. I was charged with murder and in those days, the penalty was death. I never expected to be acquitted but I held onto a faint hope.'

Mancini said he killed Violet after they argued and she came at him with a hammer which was kept by the fireplace for breaking coal. In the struggle, he snatched the hammer from her and threw it back at her. It struck her head and she fell to the floor, striking her head on a brass fender. In a rage, he had grabbed her shoulders and kept beating her head against the fender until she was dead.

Although Sussex police knew that Mancini could not be charged with a crime for which he had already been acquitted, they did re-open the case with a view to perhaps charging Mancini with perjury but they discovered that all the original documents and witness statements from the 1934 case had been destroyed by the Brighton police in 1964. Then the Director Of Public Prosecutions stepped in and ruled that due to the passage of time, there could be no independent collaboration of Mancini's confession and in a letter to the Chief Constable of Sussex, said: 'There is insufficient evidence available - or likely to become available – to prosecute Mancini for perjury.'

That statement drew the final line under the Mancini case. Or so it seemed.

Yet there was another twist in store. Two years later, after some initial correspondence with Tony Mancini, writer Stephen Knight persuaded Mancini to meet up in London to discuss the trunk murder case in more depth. The interview in May 1978 - shortly before Mancini died - was spread over three days and afterwards Mancini swore a legal affidavit before a solicitor confirming all he had said in the interview was the truth.

Mancini gave Stephen Knight a slightly different account of what happened that fateful night. He said that Violet Kaye was very jealous and that after she accused him of seeing another woman, a violent row ensued. He said she ran at him with a hammer and that as she took 'a wild swing' at him he punched her in the face and knocked her to the floor where she struck her head on a brass fender. As he stooped to help her, he said she spat in his face and he went into what he described as 'a red haze', grabbed hold of her and repeatedly banged her head against the brass fender.

Knight put it to him that it was not the accidental fall onto the fender which killed Violet but Mancini repeatedly banging her head on it, and Mancini agreed.

The confessions given to Alan Hart and Stephen Knight varied slightly in details but in both, Mancini admitted he had murdered Violet Kaye.

Despite the confessions, no action was taken against Tony Mancini. Most of the people associated with the original case were dead, the police files on the case had been destroyed, and the legal position was unchanged – no one could be tried twice for the same crime, even if they admitted it.

Officially, the death of Violet Kaye and that of the anonymous victim of the first Brighton trunk murder are classified as unsolved.

BRAINSTORM

When pretty 19-year-old Gabrielle Vallance met up with her new boyfriend Miles Giffard in a London pub, he surprised her by asking if she would marry him. But what he told her next was a much bigger surprise. He said he had just murdered his mother and father.

Of course, Gabrielle didn't believe him - she thought he was joking. But it was no joke.

Miles Giffard really had murdered his parents the previous evening and the strange and almost unbelievable reason lay 250 miles from London at the family home near St Austell in Cornwall.

The year was 1952 and Giffard was 26, good-looking, charming, public-school educated and from a wealthy family – his father Charles was a senior partner in a firm of solicitors and his mother Elizabeth was vice-chairman of the St Austell Conservative Association.

Yet despite that promising background, Miles turned out to be a feckless young man, unable to hold down a job, even a position with his father's law firm. He drank too much, squandered money and when funds ran out, stole his mother's jewellery and sold it all. The family did not report the theft and Miles was forgiven.

His fortune changed soon after when he received a legacy of £750 – about £15,000 in today's money - and he went to live in Bournemouth where it took him just four months to spend all the money and return home to St Austell flat broke. His father decided to give him an allowance of £15 a month (about £450 today) and he moved to a flat in London where he quickly found his allowance was not enough to live on, so he resorted to bouncing cheques and cadging cash off friends.

While in London, Miles met Gabrielle Vallance and was immediately captivated by her. She lived with her mother in Chelsea and both women were impressed by Miles – his natural charm, well-spoken manner and lavish generosity had quickly won them over. Miles took Gabrielle to smart restaurants and West End shows and the couple got on well, but Gabrielle was unaware that Miles had now run out of money.

Miles told her he had to return home for a few days and he set off, hitching rides to St Austell and arriving on Sunday November 2nd. He was hoping his father would advance him money but his father would not, saying he did not approve of his son's relationship with Gabrielle, and told him to end it. This was a shock set-back for Miles, who was emotionally-charged with thoughts only of Gabrielle and his desperate need to get back to her. The next day, he wrote Gabrielle a letter:

'I have had a terrible row with the old man, made worse by the fact that as usual, he is right. Anyway, the upshot is that he has forbidden me to return to London, at least for the time being. He says he will cut me off with the proverbial penny so there does not seem any alternative until I get a job.'

He went on to write: I am terribly upset and miserable as I was especially looking forward to seeing you tomorrow. Short of doing him in, I see no future in the world at all.'

What exactly happened in the Giffard household over the next couple of the days is unclear. Miles probably tried without success to persuade his father to relent, or perhaps a sense of injustice and desperation boiled within him and it reached volcanic pressure.

What is certain is that on November 7th, Miles spent the afternoon alone at the family home, a large detached house overlooking the sea. His father had gone to his office, his mother to a meeting elsewhere and their live-in maid Barbara Orchard had been given the afternoon off.

His father was the first to arrive home, at about 7.30pm. As he was parking the car – he had used his wife's Standard 8 - at the side of the house, Miles approached him and as he got out of the car, Miles attacked him with a length of iron piping, striking his father several blows and knocking him unconscious. Meanwhile, Miles's mother Elizabeth has returned home in her husband's car and unaware of what had happened at the side of the house, had gone in through the front door. Miles followed her into the kitchen and battered her with the iron pipe.

He then calmly rang Gabrielle to tell her he would be coming to see her in London the next day after all, but did not mention what he had done.

His next move was to go outside where he found Charles Giffard recovering consciousness so he clubbed him again until he was dead. Returning to the kitchen, Miles found his mother was also regaining consciousness so he struck her several more blows. As the maid was due back soon, Miles decided he needed to quickly get rid of the bodies.

He loaded his mother - who was still alive though not conscious - and his father into a wheelbarrow and pushed it the short distance to the cliff edge where he tipped them over, hoping the sea would sweep them away. He then ran back to the house and cleaned up most of the blood in the kitchen, grabbed some fresh clothing, took what cash he could find along his mother's jewellery and drove off in his father's Triumph car just as Barbara Orchard was returning - she saw him speed away.

However, even when she went into the house, she saw nothing to indicate anything was wrong.
Mr and Mrs Giffard were often out in the evening so their absence was not unusual. She noticed the kitchen floor was damp and has recently been cleaned and thought there were few traces of blood remaining but surmised there may have been an accident. She rang two local hospitals to check, but they had had no admissions involving the Giffards so Barbara went to bed.

But Barbara didn't get much sleep - she became increasingly worried as the hours passed and Mr and Mrs Giffard had not returned so at 5am, she got up and went to the house of her fiancé to seek his advice. He in turn contacted the Giffard's gardener Harry Rowe and he immediately contacted the police.

Soon, a police superintendent, a scenes-of-crime officer and the county pathologist Dr Denis Hocking were at the home of the Giffard family and it wasn't long before they began to piece together what had happened. They found the bloodstained car in the garage, and when the gardener noticed the wheelbarrow was missing, they were able to follow its wheel tracks out of the gate and along a footpath leading to the cliffs. There they found the abandoned wheelbarrow and when they looked over the cliff-edge they could see the body of Charles Giffard on the beach 120 feet below. Further along the beach they found the body of Mrs Giffard.

Dr Hocking established that Charles Giffard had died from head wounds before being tipped over the cliff and that Elizabeth Giffard was unconscious but still breathing when she was sent plummeting onto the rocks.

Meantime, Miles Giffard was already in London having driven all night, stopping only to change clothes, throwing his bloodstained clothing and the iron pipe into a river. He arrived at Gabrielle's house, saw her and her mother and acted normally, saying he had business appointment but would be back later. While away, he sold his mother's jewellery for £50 (about £1,400 today) and at 2pm met up with Gabrielle and her mother. The three then went to see the Charlie Chaplin film Limelight and after the film, Mrs Vallance went home, leaving Miles and Gabrielle together. They had drinks in a nearby pub and it was then that Miles asked her to marry him. She said she would, provided that he found a job. After a few more drinks, Miles suddenly said to her: 'I have done a frightful thing.'

'You've pinched your father's car?' she asked.

Miles calmly told her he had killed his father and mother, but Gabrielle didn't believe him and they moved on to another pub before he then took her home in a taxi. At that point he told her: 'I cannot see you anymore,' but added that he was staying at the Regency Court Hotel and he would ring her the next day.

As soon as Gabrielle was out of the taxi and it begam to move off, the police surrounded it and Miles Giffard was arrested.

The police were there because Barbara Orchard had seen Miles fleeing the scene in his father's Triumph car and it was thought he was probably heading to London. The Metropolitan Police were alerted and asked to try to locate the car, which had the distinctive registration number ERL 1. They had found the car parked in Tite Street, Chelsea where Gabrielle and her mother lived, and a number of police officers lay in wait for the couple to return.

Next morning at Canon Row police station, Miles was told enquiries were being made into the death of his parents. 'I know what you are referring to,' said Miles. 'I wish to admit everything to you with as little trouble as possible.'

He told them he did not want to involve Gabrielle and added: 'I had a brainstorm.'

Miles Giffard was formally charged with the murder of his parents and at a preliminary hearing, his legal counsel said Miles would be pleading not guilty and that his defences would be that he was insane at the time of the killings.

When the trial began on February 3rd at Bodmin Assizes, one of the first witnesses was Gabrielle Vallance who told the court that she didn't believe Miles when he told her he had murdered his father and mother as he had seemed quite normal, though she thought he was a little more quiet than usual.

Prosecuting counsel J. Scott Henderson read out the letter Giffard had sent to Gabrielle a few days earlier in which he wrote of his frustration with his father and saying there was nothing he could do about it 'short of doing him in.' The prosecutor said this phrase was clear evidence of premeditated murder and that killing of his father was not an impulsive act in a fit of temper.

Over the next two days, defence counsel John Maude called various witnesses to support the case that Giffard was insane at the time of the killings. What emerged was a tragic story of a young man who had found life difficult to handle from a very early age. When only fourteen, he had been seen by a psychiatrist who said he had a psychopathic personality, lacked normal emotions and had a rare form of schizophrenia. Miles was treated for two years, was moved to a new school and later served four years national service in the Royal Navy, where he did well.

Yet when he returned to civilian life and was being ruled by an overbearing father, he quickly deteriorated into a rather feckless young man who couldn't keep a job and was very self-centred.

The jury heard some conflicting medical evidence, for while experts including a Harley Street psychiatrist were clear that Miles had mental problems and was almost certainly in a schizophrenic state when he killed his parents, the Giffard's family doctor who had known Miles for 20 years disagreed and described him as 'an idle, selfish waster.'

Summing up, the judge Mr Justice Oliver told the jury they had to decide if Miles Giffard at the time he killed his parents knew what he was doing was wrong. He was either guilty, or he was guilty but insane - there could be no other verdict.

The jury took just 35 minutes to decide Miles Giffard was guilty of murder, and he was sentenced to death. An appeal was lodged but when the case was reviewed, the appeal was dismissed and Miles Giffard was hanged on February 24th, 1953.

A few days later, there was a poignant postscript to this unusual and distressing case – The Times newspaper published a letter from Miles Giffard's uncle, General Sir George Giffard, who had paid for his nephew's defence. In the letter he highlighted his nephew's long history of mental problems and added: 'For a jury to be expected to decide on February 6 how the mind of a man suffering from mental illness was working on the night of November 7 seems to the ordinary layman to be absurd. To decide such cases by rules which in the light of present-day knowledge are admitted to be in need of revisions seems to me to be manifestly unjust.'

Reviewing the evidence in this distressing case, I concur with the view expressed by General Sir George Giffard that the court's verdict was unjust. The very act of murdering your parents and tipping them off a cliff just because they wouldn't give you more money or forbid you to see your girlfriend is so extreme that it points to a severe mental disorder. The sheer brutality and callousness of the crime would have certainly weighed heavily on the minds of the jury, but even so, expert medical evidence had shown a history of mental problems and I think a verdict of 'guilty but insane' would have been more appropriate.

JUDGE AND JURY

When Frank Smith found out his wife was having an affair, he threatened verbally and in writing to kill the other man and having lured his intended victim to a rendezvous, he went armed with a gun and the lover was shot dead. Yet what appeared to be a clear case of wilful murder turned out to something very different and led to one of the most controversial murder trials of the 1920s.

It involved a famous and charismatic defence barrister staging a dramatic courtroom struggle with a firearms expert for possession of the murder weapon, a formidable 'hanging judge' known as The Sphinx and a case so emotionally charged, dozens of people in the courtroom were sobbing.

At the centre of this extraordinary murder trial was Alfonso Francis Austin Smith, known as Frank Smith, who was born in Toronto but educated in England where he stayed on, living in Kent with his wife Ruth. It was an unhappy marriage and in 1919, Frank, then 37, met a pretty girl called Rosina Wright who was 26 and used the first name Kathleen.

It seemed love at first sight for both of them and they lived together while Frank obtained a divorce. They married in 1925, by which time they had three children, but their happiness was to be blighted when Frank met a man called John Derham and the two struck up a friendship. Derham, who was 39, was educated at Eton, the son of a barrister, and was an England international ice-hockey player and grandson of a Victoria Cross recipient.

Derham often visited the Smiths at their home in Herne Bay in Kent and after a few months, Smith began to suspect that his wife and Derham were having an affair. Smith began to drink heavily, and confronted Derham several times, calling him 'a damned swine' and on one occasion the two men had a fist-fight, with Smith knocking out Derham.

Ordering Derham to stay away, Smith hoped that this would end the affair but it did not. Derham and Kathleen continued to meet secretly and Kathleen then instructed her lawyer to serve her husband with a deed of separation. When Smith received the document, he was furious, and wrote several letters to Derham. In one, he said: 'You dirty white-livered fool. You lied to me and now you are going to suffer.' He also wrote to his wife saying: 'I cannot go on living without you. I will deal with that damned cad Derham first. If ever I find him, I will deal with him whatever it may lead to.'

Kathleen was now living with Derham at a house in Herne Bay, but Derham thought it best to try to defuse the situation by going to stay with his mother in London, while Kathleen rented a house for her and her children in Tankerton, a village near Whitstable. She was joined a few days later by her 16-year-old sister Lillian who was to help look after the children.

The pressure on Smith was mounting and he had mentioned he might take his own life. 'I cannot live without you, and nor do I intend to,' he said in a letter to Kathleen. He became increasingly agitated and tried to arrange a meeting with her. 'If I do not hear from you by Monday, I will do something really desperate.'

Finally, Kathleen agreed he could visit her at her house in Tankerton for a discussion, a decision which was to have terrible consequences.

Ahead the meeting, Smith had borrowed a Webley service revolver and cartridges from a friend, saying he needed it for protection as he had to go to Ireland. When Smith arrived for his meeting with Kathleen, he told her of his suicidal thoughts and showed her the gun. Alarmed by the situation, Kathleen tried to placate Smith by saying she would think things over and they could have a further discussion the next day. With that, Smith and Kathleen went to bed in separate rooms.

Over the next couple of days they talked, and Kathleen, realising Smith was in a very unstable state, decided it was best to calm the situation by telling him she would end her relationship with Derham, even though that was not her intention. Smith was delighted and later, in a note to her, wrote: 'You have made me happier than I ever I hoped to be. I have been mad lately and in hell. Now you have given me glimpses of the heaven which with your help, I will leave no stone unturned to reach.'

However, later than same day Smith intercepted a letter to Kathleen from Derham which made it clear the love affair was still strong. He confronted Kathleen who admitted her love for Derham. Smith pleaded with her, but she would not relent. He wrote another letter to her in which he said: 'May God forgive me for what I am about to do, and may he forgive you, the cause of it all.'

Kathleen was unaware Smith had already sent a telegram to Derham in her name, asking him to return urgently. Derham had left immediately and arrived in Tankerton that same evening and was shocked when it was Smith who opened the door and welcomed him.

Smith admitted the ruse but said he just wanted to talk, and suggested one solution might be for all three of them to split up for three months for a cooling down period, but Derham and Kathleen refused and said they wanted to be together, and suggested it was Smith who should go away.

Smith produced his revolver and announced he was going to shoot himself but Derham leapt at him and snatched the gun from him and handed it to Kathleen who ran out of the room and hid it.

There was an uneasy tension for a while and Kathleen, anxious about the gun, slipped out to retrieve it and try to unload the cartridges. However, she could not get the gun open and Smith caught her in the kitchen soaking the gun in water hoping that might render it useless. Smith took the gun from her and put it in his pocket and far from being angry made the astonishing suggestion that he, Kathleen and Derham should go out to dinner at the Marine Hotel.

The trio had what must have been a very uneasy dinner but Kathleen and Derham were just glad that Smith was in a calmer mood and perhaps beginning to accept that his marriage was over.

That was not the case. When they got back to the house, Smith declared that he didn't want Derham staying overnight at the house, but Kathleen asked her sister Lillian to make up a bed for Derham in the spare room. Smith again said he intended to kill himself but exactly what happened next was to be at the very core of a dramatic murder trial.

The crucial incident was witnessed by a builder called James Barton who was walking past the house at the time and happened to glance through the drawing room window. Barton saw Smith standing by the window and Derham and Katheen together several feet away. He then heard a shot and saw Derham and Kathleen making a dash towards Smith, knocking him to the floor. But Barton did not see who fired the shot.

Inside the house, Lillian ran downstairs and into the drawing room. There she saw Smith pinned to the floor by Derham who was hitting him on the head with the revolver and Kathleen trying to pull Derham back. But when Derham stood up, he was clutching his stomach and he staggered out of the room to the front door, opened it and then collapsed outside on the pavement. A doctor was called and Derham was found to have a gunshot wound to his abdomen, and he was taken to a nearby nursing home. Smith had cuts to his head, but no other wounds.

The police were called and Smith handed a letter to the arresting officer saying it was intended for his wife. He added: 'I intended to shoot myself but, in the struggle, it went off and shot Derham.'

The following morning, Smith appeared before Canterbury Police Court charged with attempted murder. But later that day Derham died from the gunshot wound and when Smith next appeared in court, the charge of attempted murder was replaced with one of murder.

The prosecution argued that if Smith had shot Derham by accident while attempting to shoot himself, he had still committed a felony because (at the time) suicide was a criminal offence. It was also pointed out that Smith's claim of accidental shooting was not supported by the evidence – there was no burn mark around the bullet wound to suggest the shot was fired at close range during a struggle and that the bullet had entered Derham from behind and at a downward angle.

Smith was committed for trail at Kent assizes in Maidstone on a charge of murder though before the trial began, an inquest was held and found insufficient evidence as to who had fired the shot, or if it was by intent or accident, so an open verdict was recorded.

The trial began on November 25th, 1926 and Smith was charged with murder, with a second charge of being in possession of a firearm with intent to endanger life.

The judge in the case was Mr Justice Horace Avory, who was 75 at the time and had a long and very distinguished legal career including cases involving Oscar Wilde and another involving the Irish nationalist Sir Roger Casement, who was hung for treason.

Avory had a daunting reputation, often described as a 'hanging judge' because of the high number of murderers he had sent to the gallows. Within legal circles he was regarded as 'cold and utterly unemotional' and was also known as The Sphinx because of his austere and stone-faced countenance. He was also referred to among colleagues as Acid Drop because he often made very caustic comments to defendants, witnesses and even lawyers.

Sir Roland Oliver headed the prosecution, and Smith had managed to engage the famous defence counsel Sir Edward Marshall Hall, whose sharp mind, flamboyant style and sense of drama combined with his supreme talent for great oratory which could often persuade juries to side with the defendant.

While the defence case was that the shot had been fired accidentally during a struggle, medical and witness evidence suggested otherwise and initially Marshall Hall tried to persuade Smith to plead guilty to manslaughter which would carry a lighter sentence. Smith was reluctant to do this but Judge Avory refused to allow a manslaughter plea anyway, so Marshall Hall knew he had a very difficult task ahead of him.

Sir Roland Oliver also had a problem. There were only three people in the room at the time of the shooting – Smith, Derham and Kathleen – but he was not able to call Kathleen to give evidence as the law prevented a wife from giving evidence against her husband.

Marshall Hall got off to a good start when he gained a rather reluctant admission from the doctor who examined Derham's body that it was possible for the wound to have resulted from a struggle between the two men.

Then Oliver called the witness James Barton who had seen the struggle through the window of the house as he walked by. However, his evidence was unclear on exactly who was where at the precise moment the shot was fired. This was another plus-point for Marshall Hall.

The court also heard from the renowned firearms expert Robert Churchill who said the gun had not been fired at close range so was not discharged during a struggle between the two men. Marshall Hall wanted to counter this and managed to persuade a reluctant Churchill to join him in an extraordinary theatrical re-enactment of a struggle for possession of the gun. Marshall Hall hoped to show that the gun could have been fired accidently but while the demonstration was entertaining it did not produce any conclusive result.

Marshall Hall did not want Smith to give evidence as he felt his client's highly-strung state might not impress the jury, but Smith insisted and appeared in the witness box. What followed was a drama worthy of the West End stage.

Marshall Hall read out letters Smith had sent to his wife the day before the shooting in which he described his love for her, his anguish at the prospect of losing her and begging her to change her mind. Smith was an eloquent writer and Marshall Hall delivered the material with great power and as the court listened intently, Smith himself started to cry. The scene became so emotional that a woman juror collapsed in hysterics and the trial had to be halted for a few minutes for her to recover, Even in the public gallery, many people could be heard sobbing.

Smith, having regained his composure, told the court the gun was in the rear pocket of his trousers and as he attempted to remove it, there was a struggle and he heard a bang as the gun went off, and he was then struck on the head by Derham. He said he had not pulled the trigger and had attempted to take out the gun not to shoot Derham, but merely to prove to Derham and Kathleen that he had the means to shoot himself, as he had threatened to do.

Judge Avory then asked Smith why he had thought that tricking Derham into coming to the house might lead to a reconciliation. Smith said he had hoped to appeal to Derham's 'better nature'.
Avory was not impressed. 'After you had called him a damned swine, could you really appeal to his better nature?' he said sceptically.

When Marshall Hall concluded the defence case by addressing the jury, he told them that Smith never had any intention of killing Derham, and while he had considered taking his own life he still hoped for a reconciliation with Kathleen. Marshall Hall, in one of his most entrancing speeches, asked the jury to allow Smith the opportunity to resume 'his old happy life with the woman he loves.'

The jury may have been persuaded by Marshall Hall's fervent and dazzling oratory but Mr Justice Avory was not. In his summing up, he directed the jury's attention to Smith luring Derham to the meeting, and taking a gun with him. If he didn't intend to use it, then why was it loaded?

114

He also told the jury that had Kathleen been able to given evidence, he doubted she would have supported Smith's version of events.

Avory suggested it was difficult to conclude that the shooting was accidental and put forward his own scenario – that on realising Smith was taking out his gun, Derham had half-turned in an attempt to shield Kathleen when Smith fired, and that was why the bullet had entered the left side of Derham's body. It was a very plausible argument and comparing Avory's summary with Marshall Hall's alternative version took the jury two hours to debate and finally come to a conclusion.

When they returned to the courtroom, they found Smith not guilty of murder and not guilty of manslaughter and loud cheers were heard from the public gallery. As gun expert Robert Churchill later recalled: 'Marshall Hall, against all the scientific evidence, carried the day again.'

However, the joy at the not guilty verdicts was quickly quelled. Judge Avory was not best pleased with the jury's decisions, though he could not of course overturn their verdicts. But he did play a final ace.

He reminded the court that Smith also faced another charge, that of being in possession of a firearm and cartridges with the intention of endangering life, to which Smith had pleaded guilty.

He told Smith: 'In the view of the jury, I assume you had these with the intention of endangering the life of no other person than yourself. I must assume that,' he said with emphasis, adding: 'I have my own opinion on it.'

He clearly felt the jury's verdict was wrong and he sentenced Smith to one year in prison with hard labour, regarded as an unusually severe punishment for such an offence.

And Avory hadn't finished showing his displeasure with the jury. Normally, a murder trial jury is excused future jury service but Avory refused to grant this. 'I see no reason why they should be so excused,' he said drily.

The trial attracted intense Press coverage and it was widely reported by commentators that the jury had voted with their hearts rather than their heads. Thanks mainly to Marshall Hall, the jury had made an emotional connection with Smith, seeing him as a devoted husband

115

badly wronged by his wife's infidelity, yet still loving her.

Smith served his sentence and it is known that Kathleen visited him in prison. There were Press reports of a possible reconciliation but if there was, it must have been very brief for just a few months later, Kathleen went to live in France.

Once he was out of prison, Smith sold his story to The People newspaper. He repeated his assertion that the shooting of John Derham was accidental, and described his own life as 'a tragedy of reckless folly'.

The following year, 1928, a magazine published an article on capital punishment and inadvertently referred to Smith as a murderer – he had of course been acquitted. He sued for libel and was awarded damages of £500 (about £30,000 in today's money).

In 1937, Smith sued another magazine for libel - it had claimed he was acquitted only because he had such a good lawyer in Marshall Hall. Smith won the case and was awarded £1,000 in damages (about £60,000 in today's money).

However, the passing years had not been kind to him. He had been made bankrupt several times and has served a short prison sentence for obtaining credit while an undischarged bankrupt. He died in 1944 aged 55.

This unusual case, tragic for all three central characters, is still confusing viewed almost a century later. The only person who actually saw the shooting was Kathleen, who could not give evidence and who made no public revelation after the trial was over. While at the time, Smith was unstable and in a highly charged state and knew his wife was not coming back to him, he could well have shot John Derham deliberately and then claimed it was accidental. Equally, as he fumbled to get the gun from his pocket, it could have been fired accidentally. Despite Mr Justice Avory concerns, I think the case was not proved beyond reasonable doubt and acquittal was the correct decision. Whether the jury came to that conclusion from the facts or from sheer emotion, in my view they were correct.

I know from my journalistic experience that it all too easy to get emotionally involved in a murder trial when so much is at stake. I once covered a trial at Stafford Assizes where a young man was

116

accused of murdering his girlfriend. She had died while they were having sex on the back seat of a car and the prosecution case was that she had been strangled. The defendant claimed that any pressure on her throat was entirely accidental during the sex act.

Having listened to every detail of the case over several days, I was convinced there was sufficient doubt for him to be cleared of the charge. However, the jury was clearly less emotionally involved in the case than I was – they found the man guilty of murder and he was jailed for life!

ALSO BY NICK FLETCHER

SNAPSHOT

Snapshot is a collection of Max Slater
novellas which find the flawed private detective
caught up in six extraordinary and compelling cases,
each requiring him to push his investigative
skills – and his luck – to the limits.

They include an act of cold calculated vengeance in the sultry
heat of a Spanish holiday resort, a famous thriller writer
involved in a real- life murder in the idyllic French
and a pornographic photo the only clue to a shocking
double killing in an English seaside town.

'As an anti-hero private eye frequently out of his depth, Max
Slater commands the attention immediately as he walks the
tightrope of moral dilemma in seeking truth and justice.'

IMPERFECT DAY

Private eye Max Slater is initially reluctant to take on
a case which involves him having to decipher an
enigmatic message from a man who died 15 years earlier,
but the person asking for his help was the entrancingly
beautiful Grace and he finds her plea irresistible. Soon,
Slater finds himself taking on a psychotic millionaire who
appears to murder by proxy and who sees Slater standing
between him and a fortune in stolen diamonds.

Set mainly around Brighton on the south coast of England,
this fast-action thriller sees Max Slater once again having to
step outside the law in his quest for justice.

'Laced with barbed comments on modern life, piercing
observation of human foibles and often near-poetic imagery,
it's style is cool, distinctive and direct.'